FUKUSHIMA

For my brothers
Bernard and Declan

Seán McDonagh, SSC

Fukushima:
The End of Nuclear Energy?

the columba press

First published in 2012 by
the columba press
55A Spruce Avenue, Stillorgan Industrial Park,
Blackrock, Co. Dublin

Cover by Linda Kavanagh
Origination by The Columba Press
Printed by MPG Books Limited

ISBN 978 1 85607 784 2

Acknowledgments

I would like to thank everyone who helped in the research and development of this book. My sister Máire, Elizabeth McArdle and Pauline Connolly proofread this book a number of times and made many very helpful suggestions. I would also like to thank Patrick O' Donoghue and his colleagues at The Columba Press for their help throughout.

Contents

Introduction

Human beings have always been fascinated by energy. In Greek mythology, Prometheus was the son of Iapetus and Themis and brother of Atlas, Epimetheus and Menoetius. He used his shrewdness and intelligence to champion humankind against the often capricious behaviour of the gods. First, he tricked the gods out of the best portion of sacrificial meat and gave it to humans instead. Then, when Zeus, the God of sky and thunder, withheld fire from humankind, Prometheus stole it from him and again delivered it to humankind.

Zeus was so angry that he sent Pandora, the first woman to live with men. She was fashioned out of clay by Hephaestus and brought to life by the four winds. All the goddesses of Olympus assembled to adorn her, so that she would be very alluring to men. Despite Prometheus' warning, Epimetheus, accepted this 'gift' of Pandora from the gods. Pandora also possessed a jar. According to the myth, when, out of curiosity, Pandora opened the jar (often called Pandora's box), she released all kinds of evils which now plague humankind – pain, suffering, plagues, disease and death. By the time she was able to close the jar, all that was left inside was the virtue of hope.

Down through the centuries, humans have possessed the same desire to master energy as Prometheus. They have used coal, oil, gas, wood and water as sources of energy. Nuclear energy is the most recently discovered source of energy. It was discovered accidently in 1896 by French physicist Henri Becquerel. It seemed, initially, to be a perfect solution for the expanding energy-needs of humankind, as it appeared to deliver enormous amounts of energy at minimal cost. It was even said that it was 'too cheap to meter'. Unfortunately, this was an illusion. The accidents at Windscale in Britain (1958), Three Mile Island in the United States (1979), Chernobyl in the Ukraine (1986) and Fukushima in Japan in March 2011, remind us that this kind of energy comes with a Pandora's box full of trouble and potential disasters for humankind and all of life.

There is now a consensus in almost every nation across the globe that if nuclear weapons were used in a war, global ecosystems and many vital habitats would suffer irreversible damage. This would most probably lead to the extinction of an enormous number of species, including possibly, humankind. Most people can resonate with the response of the physicist Robert Oppenheimer (1904-67) on witnessing the first detonation of an atomic bomb. In later life he recalled being haunted by a verse from the Hindu scripture, the *Bhagavad Gita*: 'I am become death, the destroyer of worlds.' In this book, I will argue that what is called civilian nuclear power is also very dangerous from the time, uranium is mined but, more especially, during the thirty or forty years while the nuclear reactors are in operation. At the end of their lives, nuclear plants have to be decommissioned and highly toxic and radioactive waste will have to be buried in a place which will be safe for 200,000 years to prevent radioactive elements from entering the food-chain. In the wake of the accident at Fukushima Daiichi in March 2011, it is time that we recognised the destructive nature of nuclear energy and hand it back to Zeus.

Nuclear Power

Nuclear power involves the use of sustained nuclear fission in order to generate heat and electricity. The dream of producing electricity from nuclear energy began in the early years of the twentieth century. Scientists saw the possibilities of harnessing nuclear elements in order to produce electricity soon after the New Zealand-born British chemist and physicist Ernest Rutherford (1871-1937) demonstrated the existence of the nucleus in 1911. James Chadwick's (1891-1974) discovery of the neutron in 1932 marked another milestone in the quest for nuclear energy. In 1934, Frédéric (1900-1958) and Iréne Joliot-Curie (1897-1956) used neutrons to bombard radioactive materials which led to the discovery of induced-radioactivity. Further work in the 1930s by the Italian physicist Enrico Fermi (1901-1954), using slow neutrons, led to an increase in the effectiveness of induced-radioactivity.

Work in the late 1930s by a variety of scientists, including the German chemist Otto Hahn (1879-1968), Fritz Strassmann (1902-1980) and the Austrian physicists Lise Méitner (1878-1968) and Otto Robert Frisch (1904-1979) led to the discovery that a relatively small neutron could split the nucleus of the massive uranium atom into two equal pieces. This surprising result, called nuclear fission, led scientists to believe that if the fission reactions released additional neutrons, a self-sustaining nuclear chain reaction could be achieved. This controlled chain reaction process was confirmed experimentally by Frédéric Joliot-Curie in 1939, just as the Second World War was beginning in Europe.

Research into the military potential of nuclear power continued in countries such as Germany, the United Kingdom, the Soviet Union and the United States. In the 1930s, European scientists such as Enrico Fermi (1891-1964), Leó Szilárd (1898-1964) and Albert Einstein (1879-1955) had emigrated to the United States. Both Fermi and Szilárd were involved in the creation of the first reactor which became known as Chicago Pile-1. This achieved criticality on 2 December 1942. Their work was used by other scientists who were involved in the Manhattan Project which enriched uranium and built large reactors to produce plutonium. This was used to create the atomic bombs which destroyed the cities of Hiroshima on 6 August and Nagasaki three days later on 9 August 1945. The world was appalled by the extent of the carnage involved in destroying these two cities. It soon became clear that nuclear weapons had the potential to destroy huge areas of the planet and make them unsuitable for human habitation for decades or even centuries. It was clear that nuclear weapons needed to be controlled.

However, at the end of the Second World War, scientists and politicians began to promote the use of nuclear technology for peaceful rather than military purposes, though, as we will see later, there is a very close relationship between the military and civilian use of nuclear technology. On 20 December 1951, EBR-1, an experimental reactor at Arco, Idaho, became the first reactor to produce electricity. Nuclear research was heavily funded by governments in the United States, France, Canada, Germany, the United Kingdom and the Soviet Union.

A Nuclear Reactor

Nuclear reactors produce and control the release of energy through splitting the atoms of certain elements such as uranium. Pellets of uranium oxide (UO_2) are arranged in tubes to form fuel rods. These, in turn, are arranged into fuel assemblies in the reactor core. Reactors contain a moderator which is the material in the core that is used to slow down the neutrons released from fission, so that they can cause more fission. In many reactors, water is used, but heavy water (Deuterium oxide – D_2O) and graphite are used in some reactors. Then there are the control rods which are made with neutron-absorbing materials such as cadium or boron. These are inserted or withdrawn from the core in order to control the rate of reaction or, sometimes, to halt the reaction. A liquid or gas is circulated through the core to act as a coolant. In most reactors, water is used as a coolant. The central feature of many plants is the pressure vessel, made of hardened steel, which contains the reactor core and the moderator and cooling agent. The energy released in the reactor is used to generate steam to drive a turbine which, in turn, produces electricity. The final layer is called the containment building. This is the structure which is built around the reactor and pressure vessel. It is designed to protect the core from outside interference or attack, but it is also meant to protect people outside the nuclear plant from the effects of radiation, should anything go wrong inside the plant. This concrete and steel structure is often more than a metre thick.

On 8 December 1953, President Dwight D. Eisenhower delivered his now famous 'Atoms for Peace' speech at the 470th meeting of the United Nations General Assembly. After speaking about the dangers of nuclear weapons, the President called for the setting up of the UN Atomic Energy Agency. The Agency would be responsible for devising 'methods whereby this fissionable material would be allocated to serve the peaceful pursuits of mankind. Experts would be mobilised to apply atomic energy to the needs of agriculture, medicine and other peaceful activities. A special purpose organisation would be authorised to provide abundant electrical energy in the power-starved areas of the world.'[1]

---

1. http://www.iaea.org/About/history_speech.html. Accessed on 6 January 2012.

The future for the peaceful use of atomic energy looked very bright. In 1954, Lewis Strauss, who was the chairman of the United States Atomic Energy Commission, told a meeting of the National Association of Science Writers that he believed that electricity produced by nuclear reactors would be 'too cheap to meter'.

> Our children will enjoy in their homes electrical energy too cheap to meter ... It is not too much to expect that our children will know of great periodic regional famines in the world only as matters of history, will travel effortlessly over the seas and under them and through the air with a minimum of danger and at great speeds, and will experience a lifespan far longer than ours, as disease yields and man comes to understand what causes him to age.[2]

Strauss was probably speaking about hydrogen fusion power, but, at the time, most people believed he was speaking about civilian nuclear power. Unfortunately, it was a false dawn. Nuclear power has been plagued with accidents since the 1950s. This book will deal mainly with the accident which took place on 11 March 2011 at the nuclear power plant at Fukushima Daiichi, Japan, and the impact of that accident on the future of nuclear power right across the world.

2.http://en.wikipedia.org/wiki/Too_cheap_to_meter#cite_note-thisdayinquotes-1.

CHAPTER ONE

The Accident at Fukushima

In the past thirty-five years, the nuclear power industry experienced two major body blows. The accident at Three Mile Island, Pennsylvania, in 1979, stopped the expansion of nuclear power in its tracks. Seven years later, in 1986, the meltdown at Chernobyl had a devastating impact on nuclear power, right across the world. Just when a nuclear renaissance seemed on the cards, the fire and explosions in three of the six reactors at Japan's Fukushima Daiichi nuclear plant has put another nail in the coffin of nuclear power.

The sequence of events was as follows: On 11 March 2011, at 2.46 p.m., an earthquake registering 9 on the Richter scale, damaged the nuclear power plant and cut off the supply of electricity.[1] In response to the earthquake, the reactors shut down automatically. Even though the reactors had shut down, it was necessary to pump coolants around the reactor cores so that the fuel rods would not overheat. These coolants were pumped by the back-up diesel generators which kicked into action when the energy to the power station from the electricity grid was cut off. Unfortunately, at 3.30 p.m., the power plant was hit by a fifty-foot-high tsunami, which destroyed the fuel tanks for the generator.[2] At 7.30 p.m., the fuel began to meltdown. This, in turn, caused a build-up of superheated steam in Reactor 1. At 3 a.m., the Japanese government ordered Tokyo Electric Power Company to vent the reactor to relieve pressure. One hour later, pressure in the reactor had reached twice the pressure the unit was designed to withstand. By 6.50 a.m., most of the fuel had fallen to the bottom of the reactor pressure vessel. At 9.00 a.m. the following morning, workers

---

1. The scale devised by Charles Francis Richter uses a logarithm to produce magnitude values that are easily tractable: each one unit increase in magnitude corresponds to a thirty-fold increase in energy released. For example a magnitude 7 earthquake releases almost 1,000 times more energy than a magnitude 5 earthquake, *NewScientist*, 7 January 2012, p. ii.
2. Richard Gray and Michael Fitzpatrick, 'Nuclear firm was warned of tsunami risks,' *The Sunday Independent*, 20 March 2011, p. 20.

attempted to open the vents which were designed to release the radioactive vapour. The controls for opening the venting system, designed and built by General Electric, were in the reactor control room. Unfortunately, it proved impossible to open the vents, because of a total power failure.

According to *The New York Times*, there was 'a shouting match' between the company's nuclear vice-president, Sakae, and the director at the Fukushima nuclear plant, Mr Masao Yoshida. The former wanted to vent as soon as possible. The latter was sceptical about whether the venting would actually work.[3] By the time workers were in a position to try to open the vents manually, radiation levels were already too high. Reactor 1 exploded the day after the earthquake and blew the roof off the building containing the reactor. This released a plume of radioactive isotopes such as caesium and iodine into the environment. The pressure vessels also cracked, and this allowed radioactive-contaminated water to enter the Pacific Ocean.

Reactor 3 exploded on 14 March 2011 and injured eleven people. Reactor 2 was rocked by an explosion on 15 March 2011. This left a crack in the suppression chamber. Workers tried to open the vent manually at Reactor 1 many times but each time it closed.[4]

There was also a major concern that the cooling ponds where radioactive material was stored at Reactor 3 had run dry, which is why the workers tried to douse the pools with seawater to stop the rods with spent fuel from overheating. It appears that there was an explosion at Reactor 4, even though it was not operating when the earthquake struck. There was also a danger that the cooling ponds might overheat.[5] Without a coolant, the rods which contain radioactive elements, are supposed to be kept at a temperature below 25°C. Otherwise they will overheat, catch fire and, possibly, release radioactive elements into the environment. In the aftermath of the explosion, the temperature reached 60°C in

3. Hiroko Tabuchi, Keith Bradsher and Matthew S. Wald, 'In Japan Reactor Failings, Danger Signs for the US,' *The New York Times*, 18 May 2011, p. 1, 10A.
4. Ibid., p. 1.
5. David McNeill, 'Helicopters drop tonnes of seawater on stricken nuclear plant,' *The Independent*, 18 March 2011, p. 6.

pools 5 and 6, and 84°C in Reactor 4.[6] Engineers and others worked for days, in fifty-hour shifts, to bring the fires under control and to reconnect severed cables to the power grid. On a number of occasions, they had to release radioactive steam into the atmosphere, which is why food and water in the area have been contaminated.

Twice as much Radiation as Originally Claimed
By the end of October 2011, a report claimed that the Fukushima Daiichi nuclear power plant may have released twice as much radiation into the atmosphere as previously estimated, according to a study that contradicts official explanations of the accident. In a report published online, by the journal *Atmospheric Chemistry and Physics*, experts from Europe and the US estimated that the quantity of the radioactive isotope caesium-137 released at the height of the crisis was equivalent to forty-two per cent of that from Chernobyl.

Contrary to what the Japanese authorities were claiming, the report said that the Fukushima nuclear plant may have started releasing radiation before being hit by a magnitude 9 earthquake on 11 March 2011 and the arrival of the tsunami about forty-five minutes later. 'This early onset of emissions is interesting and may indicate some structural damage to the reactor units during the earthquake.'[7] Prior to this report, the company which operated the nuclear plant, Tokyo Electric Power, and the Japanese government had been claiming that the facility withstood the quake but was damaged by waves that breached its protective seawall. When the tsunami hit the plant, it knocked out the reactor's back-up electricity supply. As a result, the water cooling system was interrupted and the reactors went into meltdown.

Andreas Stohl of the Norwegian Institute for Air Research said measurements taken from a global network of sensors showed that the plant had released 36,000 terabecquerels of caesium-137

---

6. Ian Sample, 'Desperation and fear of radiation forces back workers,' *The Guardian*, 18 March 2011, p. 4.
7. Justin McCurry, 'Fukushima released "twice as much" radioactive material as first thought,' *The Guardian*, 28 October 2011, http://www.guardian.co.uk/world /2011/oct/28/fukushima-released-double-radioactive-material/print.

between 11 March and 20 March 2011. That is more than twice the 15,000 terabecquerels reported by the Japanese government. (A becquerel is a widely used unit of measurement of radioactivity.)[8]

In a telephone interview with Associated Press, Stohl, who led the study, attributed the discrepancy to the failure of Japanese authorities to include emissions that were blown out to sea.

Mistrust and Collusion Exacerbate the Problem
In a lengthy article entitled, 'Nuclear Crisis, Crippling Mistrust,' in *The New York Times*, on 12 June 2011, Norimitsu Onishi and Martin Facler gave a detailed account of the fractious and distrusting relationship between the Japanese Prime Minister, Naoto Kan's office and the management of Tokyo Electric Power Company (Tepco). Mr Kan's distrust for bureaucrats and company officers stemmed from his time as the Health Minister in the mid-1990s. At the Health Ministry, he exposed one of his own officials who knew that blood which was being used to treat haemophiliacs contained the HIV virus. As a result, hundreds of people died of AIDS. Mr Kan discovered that officials in his own department and people working for the pharmaceutical company involved knew that the blood was tainted.[9] The article claims that 'mutually suspicious relations between the prime minister's aides, government bureaucrats and company officials obstructed smooth decision-making.'[10]

The prime minister received confusing risk analysis data from the chief nuclear regulator who was an ardent supporter of nuclear power. It appears that the prime minister's office was not made aware that the plant manager was using seawater to cool the reactors. Officials at Tepco, based on a guess of the mood at the prime minister's office, ordered the plant manager to stop using seawater.[11] The manager, Masao Yoshida, did something which is extraordinarily rare in Japanese bureaucracy, he disobeyed the

8. Ian Sample, 'Desperation and fear of radiation forces back workers,' *The Guardian*, 18 March 2011, p. 4.
9. Norimitsu Onishi and Martin Fackler, 'In Nuclear Crisis, Crippling Mistrust', *The New York Times*, 12 June 2011, http://www.nytimes.com/2011/06/13/world/asia/13japan.html.
10. Ibid.
11. Ibid.

order and carried on using seawater. Experts believe that he made the right decision which prevented a more serious meltdown from taking place.

An investigation by the Rebuild Japan Initiative Foundation, carried out by a team of experts composed of thirty university professors, lawyers and journalists, found that in the hours and days immediately after the earthquake and tsunami, confusing and contradictory information was flowing between Tepco, the management at the stricken power plant and the government. This almost led to a doomsday scenario which would have engulfed even Tokyo. Tepco's president, Mr Masataka, wanted to pull all the staff out of the stricken building. This would have had a domino effect with the nuclear power plant spiralling 'out of control, releasing even larger amounts of radioactive material into the atmosphere that would in turn force the evacuation of other nearby nuclear plants, causing further meltdown'.[12]

On hearing that the company was planning to withdraw its staff from the wrecked nuclear power plant, Prime Minister Kan stormed into Tepco's headquarters in Tokyo and demanded that the staff at Fukushima stay at the plant. According to the chief secretary to the cabinet, Yukio Edano, 'if we lose Fukushima then we will lose Tokai. If that happened, it is only logical that we would also lose Tokyo itself.'[13]

Another indicator of the shambolic nature of the response to the accident was that the prime minister's office was not even aware of some of the resources which were available and which, if used, could have speeded up the official response to the accident. Among those resources was a nationwide system of radiation detectors which was known as the System for Prediction of Environmental Emergency Dose Information, commonly called Speedi. The officials at the prime minister's office did not know about this until 16 March which was five days after the disaster struck. If this had been known, it would have prevented people from fleeing north, in the belief that the radiation would

---

12. Martin Fackler, 'Japan weighed evacuating Tokyo in nuclear crisis,' *The New York Times*, 27 February, 2012.
13. Ibid.

drift southwards. Speedi projections, in fact, predicted that the radioactive plume would spread northwards. As a result of this miscommunication, many thousands of people were exposed to the very radiation from which they were fleeing.

On the day after the accident at the Fukushima Daiichi nuclear plant, thousands of residents at the nearby town of Namie gathered in the hope that they would be evacuated. They were given no guidance from Tokyo. The local officials led the residents north, believing that winter winds would be blowing south and carrying away any radioactive emissions. For three nights, while hydrogen explosions at four of the reactors spewed radiation into the air, they stayed in a district called Tsushima where the children played outside and some parents used water from a mountain stream to prepare rice. The winds, in fact, had been blowing directly toward Tsushima. Town officials would learn two months later that a government computer system designed to predict the spread of radioactive releases had been showing just that.

The weather forecasts were not published by bureaucrats in Tokyo, who were operating in a culture that sought to avoid responsibility and, above all, criticism. At first, Japan's political leaders did not know about the Speedi system and they later played down the data, apparently fearful of having to significantly enlarge the evacuation zone and acknowledge the accident's severity.

The Japanese government downplayed the risks to civilians from the explosion, so that people would not panic. Instead of calming legitimate fears about what could happen, this approach led to an erosion of public confidence in the government's ability to be truthful and honest about nuclear power. In a desperate attempt to regain public confidence, the Japanese government allowed Emperor Akihito to make a TV broadcast expressing sympathy to the victims of the earthquake and the tsunami and to voice deep concerns about the 'unpredictable' situation at Fukushima.[14]

---

14. Tania Branigan, 'Radiation leak thwarts bid to regain control of reactors,' *The Guardian*, 17 March 2011, p. 2.

As a result of the Japanese government's failure to give clear and honest information about what had happened, and what the consequences might be, the normally stoic Japanese citizens were outraged. According to *The Mainichi Daily News*, 'residents who have been evacuated after a radiation leak from a quake-hit nuclear power plant have expressed their anger with the lack of information about the incident and how to respond to it.'[15]

Reassurances from governments and the nuclear industry in the wake of accidents at reactors were not credible. Alexey Yablokov, a member of the Russian Academy of Sciences and advisor to President Gorbachev, warns people that when you hear 'no immediate danger' (from nuclear radiation) then you should run away as far and as fast as possible.[16]

Because the government had failed to warn them of real dangers, many people tried to protect themselves. In *The New York Times* on 31 July 2011, Ken Belson wrote about Kiyoko Okoshi, who spent $625 buying a dosimeter (which measures an individual's exposure to radioactive elements in the environment) because she did not believe what the government agencies were saying about levels of radioactivity. Officials kept telling her that even though their village was in the twenty mile zone from the crippled Fukushima Daiichi nuclear power plant, there was no danger, since the village was so isolated. She used the dosimeter to check roads and woods in her village. When she checked a sewage ditch, 'the meter beeped wildly, and the screen read 67 microsieverts per hour, a potentially harmful level.'[17] (Millisieverts [mSv] are measurements of ionising radiation absorbed by a human body.) She was not the only one to have bought a dosimeter. Even in Tokyo, which is one hundred and fifty miles south of Fukushima, people, especially mothers, were testing for radioactive materials. Ken Belson made the point that dosimeter measurements by amateurs are considered crude because they measure only one kind of

15. http://www.prisonplanet.com/massive-cover-up-of-radiation-levels-in-fukushima-prefecture.html. Accessed on 26 March 2011.
16. John Vidal, 'Nuclear's green cheerleaders forget Chernobyl at our peril,' *The Guardian*, 2 April 2011, p. 38.
17. Ken Belson, 'Doubting assurances, Japanese find radioactivity on their own,' *The New York Times*, 31 July 2011.

radiation and they do not take into account the length of time the person taking the readings remained in the same place. However, in the case of Mrs Okoshi's readings, Mr Kazuyoshi Sato, a local politician who had always opposed the nuclear industry, said that Mrs Okoshi's findings were confirmed by a map of air and soil readings made by the United States Department of Energy and the Japanese government.[18] Experts point out that radioactive materials do not follow in neat patterns. The reason for this is that the direction and velocity of the wind can change, and the unique features of a landscape could mean that one place would be heavily hit by radiation whereas a nearby village could have little radiation.

The Withholding of Information was Akin to 'Murder'[19]

The New York Times found that in interviews and public statements, some current and former government officials admitted that Japanese authorities engaged in a pattern of withholding damaging information and denying some facts of the nuclear disaster. One of the reasons for this is that they wished to limit the size of costly and disruptive evacuations in land-scarce Japan. In addition, they wanted to avoid a situation where the public would question the politically powerful nuclear industry. As the nuclear plant continued to release radiation, some of which had already slipped into the nation's food supply, public anger grew at what many there saw as an official campaign to play down the scope of the accident and the potential health risks.[20]

Goshi Hosono, the minister in charge of the nuclear crisis, dismissed accusations that political considerations had delayed the release of the early Speedi data. He said that the data was not disclosed because it was incomplete and inaccurate, and that he was presented with comprehensive data for the first time only on 23 March 2011. Given the poor record of the government, many people simply did not believe him.

---

18. Ibid.
19. Norimitsu Onishi and Martin Fackler, 'Japan Held Nuclear Data, Leaving Evacuees in Peril,' *The New York Times*, 8 August 2011. http://www.nytimes.com/2011/08/09/world/asia/09japan.
20. Ibid.

The New York Times has drawn attention to the fact that the meltdowns at three of Fukushima Daiichi's six reactors went officially unacknowledged for months. In early June 2011, in one of the most damning admissions, nuclear regulators said that inspectors had found tellurium-132, which experts call telltale evidence of reactor meltdowns, a day after the tsunami but did not tell the public for nearly twelve weeks. For months after the disaster, the government flip-flopped on deciding what level of radiation was permissible in school grounds. This indecision caused confusion and anguish about the safety of schoolchildren in Fukushima.[21]

Many observers believe that the Japanese government and regulator only began to inform the public accurately about the scale of the accident when inspectors from the International Atomic Energy Agency (IAEA) discovered what had happened and were about to make a report on it. On 4 July, the Atomic Energy Society of Japan, a group of nuclear scholars and industry executives, said, 'It is extremely regrettable that this sort of important information was not released to the public until three months after the fact, and only then in materials for a conference overseas.'[22]

The group added that the authorities had yet to disclose information regarding the water level and the temperature inside the reactor pressure vessels and that this information would give a much fuller picture of the damage. Other experts said that the government and Tokyo Electric Power Company, Tepco, had failed to reveal crucial data from the power station. This information could have shed light on whether the reactor's cooling system was actually destroyed by the forty-five-foot-tall tsunami, as officials have maintained, or whether damage from the earthquake also played a role. If it is the latter, then these findings would raise doubts about the safety of other nuclear plants in a nation as seismically active as Japan.

Critics, as well as the increasingly sceptical public, seem unconvinced. They compare the response to the Minamata case in the 1950s, a national scandal in which bureaucrats and industry officials colluded to protect economic growth by hiding the fact

21. Ibid.
22. Ibid.

that a chemical factory was releasing mercury into Minamata Bay in western Japan. The mercury led to neurological illnesses in thousands of people living in the region. 'If they wanted to protect people, they had to release information immediately,' said Reiko Seki, a sociologist at Rikkyo University in Tokyo and an expert on the cover-up of the Minamata case. 'Despite the experience with Minamata, they didn't release Speedi.'

The confusion and poor decision-making in the immediate aftermath of the accident, strained the relationship between Japan and the US. The US was worried about the impact of radiation on the 50,000 military personnel stationed in Japan. Initially, the Japanese rebuffed offers from the US to help in the management of the crisis. Personnel from the United States Nuclear Regulatory Commission were in Tokyo within forty eight hours of the accident happening. They had independent verification of the seriousness of the accident from aircraft and satellites which the US ordinarily uses to gather data on North Korea. Despite their willingness to help, the US officials found it difficult to arrange meetings with their counterparts in Tokyo, until the Obama administration began to put pressure on the Kan administration. All of this shows that, despite the technical prowess and sophisticated society of the Japanese people, mistrust, collusion and poor communications between the government, the operating company and the management at the plant exacerbated an already serious situation and they were very lucky that a complete meltdown did not happen.

In August 2011, the Japanese government made an important decision to move the country's nuclear safety agency from under the aegis of the trade ministry. The trade ministry is also tasked with promoting and expanding the use of nuclear power stations. It is clear there was a major conflict of interest between ensuring safety, and, at the same time, promoting the nuclear industry. The nuclear safety agency is now housed at the environment ministry where, an editorial in *The Guardian* believed that 'at least in theory there is some chance that its operation will not be subverted or manipulated by Japanese energy firms.'[23]

23. 'After Fukushima – Nuclear dirty tricks,' editorial, *The Guardian*, 16 August 2011, p. 30.

The editorial draws attention to the appallingly manipulative behaviour of energy companies such as Kyushu Electric Power Company. Their workers were told to pose as ordinary concerned citizens and to send emails to a televised public hearing demanding a resumption of operation at two nuclear reactors in southern Japan. The most damning revelation is that the nuclear agency itself was also engaged in these dirty trick manoeuvres. The author of the editorial believes that such tactics are not confined to Japan. It claims that 'the same factors are at work in every country that has a nuclear industry. The impulse to minimise the inherent risks of the most dangerous technology man has ever tried to master, the tendency to conceal or downplay accidents, the assertion that each succeeding generation of plants is foolproof and super safe, and the presumption, so often proved wrong by events, that every contingency has been provided for, all of these have been evident again and again.'[24]

A Japanese government report in October 2011 accepted that it would take thirty years to decommission the four crippled nuclear reactors at the Fukushima Daiichi nuclear power plant.[25] The draft report, released by Japan's Atomic Energy Commission of the Cabinet Office on Friday 28th, said the removal of debris – or nuclear fuel – should begin by the end of 2021. 'We set a goal to start taking out the debris within a ten-year period, and it is estimated that it would take thirty years or more (after the cold shutdown) to finish decommissioning because the process at Fukushima would be complicated,' the report states.[26]

Cold Shutdown by the End of 2011

By December 2011, experts were asking whether the cold shutdown of the stricken reactors which was scheduled to occur before the end of the year would actually happen. The term 'cold shutdown' is a technical term which is used to describe intact reactors with

---

24. Ibid.
25. From Junko Ogura, 'Japan: Damaged reactors at nuclear plant could take 30 years to retire,' http://edition.cnn.com/2011/11/01/world/asia/japan-nuclear/index.html.
26. Ibid.

fuel cores that are in a safe and stable condition.[27] Lazuhiko Kudo, a professor of nuclear engineering at Kyushu University, believes that the Japanese government is more concerned with appeasing the growing public anger than with telling people the whole truth. The term 'cold shutdown' gives an exaggerated impression that the severely damaged reactors are under control and everything will be safe.

Noboru Nakao, a nuclear engineering consultant at International Access Corporation, says that 'claiming a cold shutdown does not have much meaning for damaged reactors like those at Fukushima Daiichi.'[28] With help from American, French and Japanese companies, a new cooling system has been completed which has managed to cool the reactors' cores along with the molten fuel which is attached to the outer containment vessels. But a severe earthquake in the region could knock out or severely damage this new cooling system and could set off another chain reaction, since the system was not built to earthquake safety standards.[29]

These same experts agreed, however, that the cover which has been built at Unit 1 reactor building has helped reduce radiation leaks into the atmosphere.

The Japanese government's focus on cold shutdown also deflected attention away from other issues such as the 90,000 tonnes of nuclear-contaminated water that is still either in the basements of the stricken reactors or is stored in tanks around the plant. This water is still posing a threat to the Pacific Ocean, especially off the coast of Japan.

Fukushima Investigation Reveals Failings
In December 2011, a 507-page interim report found that the response to the nuclear crisis and the tsunami was confused and quite incompetent. The report painted a picture of harried workers and government officials scrambling to respond to the problem. The

---

27. Martin Fackler, 'Japan May Declare Control of Reactors, Over Serious Doubts,' *The New York Times*, 14 December 2011. http://www.nytimes.com/2011/12/15/world/asia/japan-set-to-declare-control-over-damaged-nuclear-reactors.html.
28. Ibid.
29. Ibid.

authorities had only prepared for a six-metre-high tsunami, whereas the tsunami was twice that height. The report criticised the use of the term *soteigai*, meaning unforeseeable, which implied that authorities were shirking responsibility for what had happened by labeling the events as beyond their expectations.[30]

One of the most serious findings of the report for the nuclear industry, both in Japan and worldwide, was the fact that many of the workers at Tokyo Electric Power Company (Tepco) were 'untrained to handle emergencies such as the power shutdown that struck when the tsunami destroyed the back-up generators, thus setting off the nuclear disaster.'[31] There was no clear manual outlining what ought to be done in these circumstances. There was very poor communication among the staff and between the operator and the government. One consequence of this poor communication was that it took hours to find any alternative way to bring seawater to cool the reactor and prevent the meltdown. The report stated that: 'A better response might have reduced the core damage, radiation leaks and the hydrogen explosions that followed at two reactors and sent plumes of radiation into the air.'[32]

Japan Recommends Temporary State Control for Tokyo Electric
On 27 December 2011, the Japanese government told Tokyo Electric Power Company to consider ceding control of the company to the Japanese government in exchange for much-needed funds to deal with the fallout from the nuclear accident at Fukushima in March 2011. It is estimated that the company needs 689.4 billion yen or US$8.8 billion to make the plant safe and compensate the 100,000 people who had fled their homes, with little prospect of returning for a number of decades.[33]

30. Associated Press 'Japanese government delayed giving information to the public, according to an interim report into the disaster,' *The Guardian*, 26 December 2011. http://www.guardian.co.uk/world/2011/dec/26/fukushima-investigation-reveals-failings/print.
31. Ibid.
32. Ibid.
33. By Hiroko Tabuchi, 'Japan Recommends Temporary State Control for Tokyo Electric,' *The New York Times*, 27 December 2011. http:// www.nytimes.com /2011/12/28/business/global/japan-recommends-temporary-state-control-for-tokyo-electric.html.

It appears that the company will have to decommission all the six reactors at Fukushima Daiichi and not just the four which were affected by the earthquake and tsunami. Tokyo Electric Power's president, Toshio Nishizawa, said the company would seriously consider various possibilities because the company wanted to ensure that it never let such an accident happen again.

CHAPTER TWO

The Fallout

Within two weeks of the explosions at Fukushima, radioactive iodine-131 was detected in the water supply of Tokyo, even though the nuclear plant is 140 miles north of the city. Officials in Japan's Health Ministry warned parents not to allow infants to drink the water because levels of iodine-131 had been detected at 201 becquerels per litre. The recommended level for adults is 300 becquerels and for infants it is 100 becquerels per litre. Children are more susceptible to radiation because, as they are growing up, their thyroid glands are more active and, as a result, they need more iodine.[1] Radioactive iodine-131 has a half-life of eight days. In order to calculate how long an isotope such as iodine-131 retains its radiation, one multiplies the number eight by twenty, which means it is radioactive for approximately 160 days.[2] There are about 80,000 children living in the affected area. Humans are exposed to this radioactive isotope both by breathing it in or by eating or drinking food which has been contaminated. For example, when cows eat grass which has been polluted with iodine-131, it is concentrated in their milk and absorbed into the blood stream when children drink the contaminated milk. Iodine-131 is absorbed by the thyroid gland at the base of the neck. Higher than normal or acceptable levels of radioactive material were found in many vegetables in the Fukushima Prefecture.

Two weeks after the disaster, Japan's Nuclear Safety Commission encouraged people to evacuate from a much wider area from the site of the nuclear accident. The Japanese government admitted that part of the Fukushima nuclear plant was so damaged by the earthquake that it would be difficult to bring it under control quickly. The new evacuation area recommended by the Japanese government covered a zone extending to nineteen miles from the

---

1. Helen Caldicott, 'Nuclear Power is Not the Answer,' *The New Press*, New York, 2006, p. 47.
2. David Jolly and Denise Grady, 'Tokyo Says Radiation in Water Puts Infants at Risk,' *The New York Times*, 23 March 2011. www. nytimes.com/2011/03/24/word /asia/24/japan/html.

damaged reactor. The US government was recommending that their citizens stay at least fifty miles from the stricken plant. It also seemed that there had been a crack in the containment vessel in Reactor 3. This raised the radioactive levels in the water where officials were working to 10,000 times above the normal level in water at the plant.[3] By 30 March 2011, experts were saying that, given the increased levels of radiation, it appeared that the radioactive core at Reactor 2 had melted through its containment vessel and escaped onto the concrete floor.[4]

On 4 April 2011, the Japanese government broke its own rules by releasing 11,500 tonnes of contaminated water into the Pacific Ocean. This was to make space for the storage of highly radioactive water which was contaminated when seawater was used to cool the damaged reactors and cooling ponds. The radioactive water which was discharged into the sea was one hundred times above the legal limit, but the Japanese authorities justified their action by claiming that it was necessary in order to allow the workers to contain some of the more severe leaks. The chief cabinet secretary, Yukio Edano, told reporters, 'We didn't have any other alternative. This is a measure we had to take to secure safety.'[5]

Water and Food Contamination

According to Ken Belson and Hiroko Tabuchi of *The New York Times*, this bad news from Fukushima undermined the optimistic statements by government and company officials.[6] On 30 March 2011, scientists found high levels of caesium-137 in soil samples in Litate, a village of 7,000 people about twenty-five miles north-west of Fukushima. The half-life of caesium is thirty years, which makes it harmful for six hundred years. It is concentrated in fish

3. Hiroko Tabuchi Keit Bradsher and David Jolly, 'Japan Encourages a Wider Evacuation from Reactor Area,' *The New York Times*, 25 March 2011, www.nytimes.com/2011/03/26/world/asia/26japan.html.

4. Ian Sample and Allegra Stratton, 'Race to save Fukushima reactor is lost, says expert,' *The Guardian*, 30 March 2011, p. 1.

5. Jonathan Watts, 'Japan to discharge radioactive water into the Pacific,' *The Guardian*, 5 April 2011, p. 14.

6. Ken Belson and Hiroko Tabuchi, 'Confidence Slips Away as Japan Battles Nuclear Peril,' *The New York Times*, http://www.nytimes.com/2011/03/30/world/asia/30japan.html.

and animal tissues and is readily deposited in human muscles where it irradiates the muscle cells and other organs. It is very carcinogenic.[7]

After the explosions at Fukushima, caesium-137 levels were about double the minimums found in an area declared uninhabitable around the Chernobyl nuclear plant in Ukraine. This raises the question as to whether the evacuation zones around Fukushima should be extended beyond the current nineteen miles. On Thursday 29 March 2011, the Japanese government said it had no plans to expand the zone.[8]

On 30 March 2011, the Japanese ministry of agriculture published data on radioactive contamination. It stated that caesium-137, was found at 2,200 times the normal level in soils about forty kilometres from the Fukushima plant. Small quantities of plutonium have been found in soil close to the stricken nuclear plant. It is thought that the contamination came from the melted fuel rods at the nuclear reactor. Radioactive iodine registering 3,555 times the safe limit was detected in the ocean three hundred metres from the plant.[9] The high levels of radiation raise concerns that fish, shellfish and seaweed, which form part of the Japanese diet, could cause harm to humans who eat these marine products.[10]

In the autumn of 2011, government inspectors came to check for levels of radioactive contamination of rice in the Onami Valley which is located about thirty-five miles north-west of the Fukushima Daiichi reactors. The inspectors declared that Onami rice was safe for human consumption even though they only tested two rice farms out of one hundred and fifty-four farms. Not everyone was convinced by the clean bill of health from the government inspectors, so one sceptical farmer decided to have his own rice tested. When the results came back, the rice contained levels of caesium-137 which were above the government's

7. Helen Caldicott, op. cit., p. 64.
8. Henry Fountain, 'Cleanup Questions as Radiation Spreads' The New York Times, 1 April 2011, http://www.nytimes.com/2011/04/01/world/asia/01clean.html.
9. David McNeill, 'Japan to decommission four of six nuclear reactors,' The Irish Times, 31 March 2011, p. 13.
10. Ian Sample, 'Radiation could harm Japan's marine life,' The Guardian, 31 March 2011, p. 23.

safety limits.[11] Other farmers began to have their rice tested and, in each case, unsafe levels of caesium were found. To avoid panic, the government promised to test more than 25,000 farms in the eastern Fukushima Prefecture close to where the accidents took place. According to Mitsuhiro Kukao, an economics professor at Keio University in Tokyo, 'Since the accident, the government has tried to continue its business-as-usual approach of understating the severity of the accident and insisting that it knows best.'[12] The government has lost a lot of credibility because it is underestimating the damage caused by the meltdown at the nuclear plant.

Because people no longer trust the government to tell them the truth, more than a dozen radiation-testing stations, which are operated mainly by volunteers, have sprung up around Fukushima and even as far south as Tokyo. Some of the testing equipment costs approximately $40,000 and the operators claim that their results are more accurate and transparent than tests by government agencies. The results can be devastating for some farmers. *The New York Times* correspondent, Martin Fackler, spoke to a Mr Muto who had lost all his mushroom crop, totalling 110,000 mushrooms, because the test revealed a high level of radiation. Because Mr Muto is not living in the exclusion zone around the crippled nuclear reactors, the operators of the plant, Tepco, have not offered full compensation to farmers outside the twelve mile zone. The future seems very bleak indeed for many of the farmers in the Onami valley. Many of these farmers are distraught as their ancestors have farmed in this area for generations. Some shops, such as the newly-opened Vegetable Café Harmonize, advertise the fact that their food comes only from western Japan, far away from the source of the problem. People who traditionally bought local food are now buying food at this shop because they wish to protect themselves and their children from contaminated food products and they have lost faith in the truthfulness of the

---

11. Martin Fackler, 'Japanese Struggle to Protect Their Food Supply,' *The New York Times*, 21 January 2012, http://www.nytimes.com/2012/01/22/world/asia/wary-japanese-take-food-safety-into-their-own-hands.html.
12. Ibid.

government. According to Sachiko Sato, 'If the government treated us like adults, there would be no need for these new stores.'[13]

On 11 April 2011, the Japanese nuclear regulatory agency raised its assessment of the seriousness of the crisis at Fukushima Daiichi nuclear power plant from five to seven. This signifies a major accident, which put it on a par with Chernobyl, and was an admission that the release of radioactive elements will have substantial and long-lasting consequences for health and for the environment. Since the crisis began, environmental groups such as Greenpeace and independent scientists have been saying that a large amount of radiation had been released, even though Japanese officials had played down the seriousness of the accident. On the same day, 11 April 2011, Hidehiko Nishiyama, the deputy-director general of Japan's nuclear regulatory agency, admitted that the total amount of radiation released so far was about ten per cent of what was released after the Chernobyl accident. But, at a separate news conference, an official from Tokyo Electric said, 'The radiation leak has not stopped completely and our concern is that it could eventually exceed Chernobyl.'[14]

The accident at Chernobyl involved a burning graphite reactor which spewed radioactive particles into the atmosphere. These elements were carried across Western Europe by winds. In contrast, the Fukushima accident had produced radioactive water run-off into the Pacific Ocean. According to Professor Tetsuo Iguchi, from the Department of Quantum Engineering at Nagoya University, 'The fact that we have now confirmed the world's second-ever level 7 accident will have huge consequences for the global nuclear industry. It shows that current safety standards are woefully inadequate.'[15] In response to the new ratings, the Japanese authorities have ordered people living within a twelve-mile radius of the plant to leave their homes. People within a nineteen-mile radius were advised to stay indoors.

By the beginning of June 2011, it became clear that the amount of radiation released by the accident at the Fukushima Daiichi nuclear plant was double the amount initially estimated by the

---

13. Ibid.
14. Ibid.
15. Ibid.

operators. Scientists now believe that 770,000 terabecquerels of radiation seeped from the power plant in the week after the earthquake. This is about twenty per cent of the estimated figure for Chernobyl after the accident there.[16]

Radiation levels have seriously damaged wildlife. Researchers Timothy Mousseau, a biological scientist at the University of South Carolina in the US, and Anders Pape from Denmark, found that the radiation from the Fukushima Daiichi accident has affected birdlife. It has reduced the longevity of birds and affected avian male fertility. They analysed fourteen species of birds from around Chernobyl and Fukushima. According to the research, many species showed 'dramatically' elevated DNA mutation rates and development abnormalities.[17] According to their study, the impact of the Fukushima Daiichi disaster was worse than the Chernobyl accident.

More Damage to Reactors than Expected
On 12 May 2011, Tepco admitted that the damage to reactor No. 1, was much more serious than originally stated. Tepco had suspected that the containment vessels at two of the reactors had been breached but they had hoped that the No. 1 reactor was intact. On 12 May 2011, workers who were able to monitor water levels in the reactor found that they were much lower than they expected. One of the most frightening findings 'was that the water levels in the reactor vessel, which housed the fuel rods, was about three feet below where the bottom of the rods would normally stand'.[18] It now seems that the fuel rods were uncovered early on in the crisis, before tonnes of water were poured in to try to keep the rods cool. Tepco spokesperson, Junichi Matsumoto, told a news conference that the fuel had melted and slumped to the bottom of the vessel in little pellets. Experts feared that such a scenario would allow the chain reaction to re-ignite with potentially catastrophic consequences

16. Justin McCurry, 'Nuclear agency raises new Fukushima radiation fears,' *The Guardian*, 8 June 2011, p. 18.
17. David McNeill, 'Bird life badly hit by nuclear fallout in Japan,' *The Irish Times*, 3 February 2012, p. 12.
18. Hiroko and Matthew L. Wald, 'Damage at a Japanese Reactor Is Worse Than Expected,' *The New Yorker*, 13 March 2011, p. A8.

because of the release of large quantities of radioactive material. David Lochbaum from the Union of Concerned Scientists said that 'he believed that the damage to the fuel at Reactor 1 was finished, and even if some fuel rods were still standing and therefore exposed – they were no longer hot enough to keep melting.'[19] He cautioned that things could get worse if the continued addition of water facilitated conditions for a nuclear reaction.[20]

Panic and Incompetence

Before the in-depth reports on what actually happened at the Fukushima nuclear power plant, many people would have argued that the Japanese people were one of the best-trained populations in the world when it came to dealing with earthquakes. The building code is rigorous and in every institution there are regular drills about how to respond to earthquakes and tsunamis. The social patterns and Japanese culture is normally one of compliance, where the people believe what their government says and follow their instructions. Yet, the incompetent way in which the Japanese authorities set about responding to the emergency at Fukushima was unbelievable. This raises serious questions about having nuclear power in countries which do not have the technical expertise, nor the organised emergency drills of the Japanese.

Lack of Proper Clothing

Unfortunately, having technical competence on paper does not mean that everything will work according to plan when there is an emergency. In an exclusive article in *The Sunday Telegraph* (27 March 2011), Andrew Gilligan and Robert Mendick interviewed some of the members of the emergency team who tried to put out the fires at the stricken Fukushima plant and reconnect the reactors to outside power cables. One of the team told the reporters that the scene at the nuclear facility was much worse than they had expected. 'Everything was covered in rubble.'[21] It would appear that those who worked at the damaged plant were not issued with

19. Ibid.
20. Ibid.
21. Andrew Gilligan and Robert Mendick, 'Fukushima fifty in their own words,' *The Sunday Telegraph*, 27 March 2011, p. 17.

the proper clothing to protect them from radiation. While all the workers had respirators, the majority wore only orange boiler suits. Only a few of the senior management team wore the proper lead-lined 'Noddy suits'. Those in the front line of danger had only disposable overalls made of Tyvek, an artificial, non-rip fibre. In Britain, those who apply spray paints and use industrial cleaners wear these garments. The reporters found that many of the workers did not believe the assurances which they were given by the authorities about the radiations levels to which they were exposed.[22]

A Preponderance of Casual and Untrained Workers at Nuclear Power Plants

One thing which those promoting nuclear power would like us to believe is that the people involved in the industry are extremely competent and trained to the highest standards. As the search-light of publicity focused on the Fukushima accident, it became clear that this is not true. *The New York Times* interviewed a Mr Ishizawa, who is one of the thousands of untrained, itinerant, temporary labourers who handle much of the dangerous work at nuclear power installations. These people are not specialists and are not even employees of Tepco. Yet, it has been revealed that they were subjected to radiation levels about sixteen times as high as the levels which were faced by the company's employees.[23] 'This is the hidden world of nuclear power,' said Yuko Fujita, a former physics professor at Keio University in Tokyo and a longtime campaigner for improved labour conditions in the nuclear industry. 'Wherever there are hazardous conditions, these labourers are told to go. It is dangerous for them, and it is dangerous for nuclear safety.'[24] The Japanese nuclear regulator admitted that in the year ending in March 2010, roughly 83,000 workers or eighty-eight per cent of the staff at Japan's eighteen commercial nuclear power plants were contract workers. At the Fukushima Daiichi plant,

22. Ibid.
23. Hiroko Tabuchi, 'Japanese Workers Braved Radiation for a Temp Job,' 9 April 2011, www.nytimes.com/2011/04/10/ world/asia/10workers.html.
24. Ibid.

eighty-nine per cent of the 10,303 workers during that same period were contract workers.'[25]

In Japan's nuclear industry, operators like Tokyo Electric have an elite corps of permanent workers who build and maintain nuclear plants. The rest of the workers, who perform difficult tasks, come from contractors and subcontractors. The wages and benefits of these workers are only a fraction of what is paid to the elite. There is also much less concern or inclination to protect these casual workers from radiation.

When disaster strikes, these casual workers do earn higher wages. Take the case of Mr Ishizawa who lived about a mile from the power station. He was offered $350 for just two hours work in the week following the disaster. This was more than twice his former pay for the week. He told *The New York Times* that some of the former members of his team had been offered nearly $1,000 a day. Offers have fluctuated depending on the progress at the plant and the perceived radiation risks that day. So far, Mr Ishizawa has refused to return.[26]

On 13 May 2011, a man died at the Fukushima Daiichi plant, about fifty minutes after beginning work. The man was in his sixties and was exposed to 0.17 millisieverts of radiation. The maximum level of exposure for male workers is 250 millisieverts for 'the duration of the effort to bring it [the reactor] under control'.[27] At a press conference on 11 May 2011, Goshi Mosono, an adviser to Prime Minister Naoto Kan, admitted that working conditions at the plant were poor. He added: 'I would like to spend my energy to improve working conditions. Many people told us that the working environment [at the plant] is way too bad.'[28]

The Fukushima nuclear emergency is particularly worrying for the worldwide nuclear industry for a number of other reasons. Japan, one of the most highly-industrialised societies on earth, is well-endowed with people highly-specialised in nuclear physics and engineering. The spectre of Japan being almost powerless in

---

25. Ibid.
26. Ibid.
27. 'Man dies at Japanese nuclear plant,' *The Irish Times*, 14 May 2011, http://www.irishtimes.com/newspaper/breaking/2011/0514/breaking3_pf.html.
28. Ibid.

the face of the disaster will not vanish quickly. The television footage of helicopters attempting and, at times, failing to dump water on the reactors will raise serious questions about the technology, in the eyes of many people. If Japan, with its technological prowess, has escaped nuclear disaster by the skin of its teeth, what chance would countries with less scientific and technological backgrounds have in the face of a nuclear meltdown?

On 30 April 2011, *The New York Times* revealed that Toshiso Kosoka, a senior advisor to the prime minister on nuclear matters, had resigned. He accused the Japanese government of ignoring his advice and failing to follow the law. Professor Toshiso Kosoka, who teaches at Tokyo University, had been appointed in March 2011. In a tearful resignation press conference, he claimed that the government had only used 'flexible approaches' to laws and regulations and only 'stop-gap measures' that were 'delaying the end' of the nuclear crisis.[29] On 19 May 2011, Toshio Nishizawa, the managing director of Tepco, was forced to resign as a result of the company's mishandling of the Fukushima crisis. The accident has already cost the company 1.25 trillion yen ($15 billion). This is a record loss for a Japanese company outside the financial and banking sector.[30]

Japan Cancels Plans to Build more Nuclear Power Plants
On 10 May 2011, the Japanese Prime Minister, Naoto Kan, said that Japan would abandon plans to build more nuclear reactors, saying that 'his country needs to start from scratch in creating a new energy policy'.[31] Before the Fukushima disaster, Japan had planned to build fourteen nuclear reactors by 2030. This would have increased the nuclear segment in Japan's electricity production to fifty per cent. A few days before this announcement, the prime

---

29. 'Japan: Senior Nuclear Adviser Resigns, Lambasting Government's Response to Crisis,' *The New York Times*, 30 April 2011, p. A4.
30. By Tsuyoshi Inajima and Michio Nakayama, 20 May 2011, http://www.bloomberg.com/news/print/2011-05-20/tepco-president-resigns-after-utility-reports-record-15-b.
31. Martin Fackler, 'Japan to Cancel Plan to Build More Nuclear Plants,' *New York Times*, 12 May 2011, page A8. Matthew L. Wald contributed from Washington and Andrew Pollack from Los Angeles.

minister had stated that Japan remained committed to nuclear
power. The speculation is that the U-turn came in the wake of
public opinion which 'has significantly soured on nuclear power
since the Fukushima accident'.[32] The prime minister vowed that
the two new pillars of Japan's energy policy would be renewable
energy and conservation.

As a result of the accident at Fukushima, Tepco halted construction at its Higashidori plant and also suspended plans for
three more units. Two other Japanese power companies have also
taken similar actions. Electric Power Development Co. stopped
construction at its Oma plant and Chubu Electric postponed the
construction of a new nuclear power plant.[33]

Other nuclear power plants are also causing concern in Japan.
The Hamaoka nuclear plant straddles two major geological
faults. Chubu Electric Power Company, which operates the plant,
told the media that it would close two out of the five reactors after
being asked to do so by Prime Minister Naoto Kan. He believes
that there is a good possibility that an earthquake of 8 on the
Richter scale will hit the area within the next thirty years. In 2004,
Katsuhiko Ishibashi, a seismologist at Kobe University, compared
Hamaoka to a kamikaze terrorist waiting to explode. Two of the
five reactors are already mothballed and another one has been
closed by inspection.[34]

On 12 July 2011, Prime Minister Naoto Kan said that Japan
should reduce its dependence on nuclear energy and eventually
stop using nuclear energy completely. He acknowledged that his
current position represents a radical shift in Japan's energy policy.
The reason he has changed his position is that he now realises in
the wake of the Fukushima accident, that nuclear energy is dangerous.
According to him, 'When we think of the magnitude of the risks
involved with nuclear power, the safety measures we previously
conceived are inadequate.'[35] Implementing this radical change

32. Ibid.
33. www.worldwatch.org/nuclear-power-after-fukushima, p. 39.
34. 'Kamikaze plant closed,' *NewScientist*, 14 May 2011, p. 4.
35. Hiroko Tabuchi, 'Japan Premier Wants Shift Away From Nuclear Power,' *The New York Times*, 12 July 2011, http://www.nytimes. com/201/07/14/world/asia/14japan.html.

will not be easy because in 2011 nuclear energy made up thirty per cent of Japan's energy needs, and the pre-Fukushima plan was to increase that to fifty per cent by the year 2030. Public opinion at the moment is quite critical of nuclear energy. A poll published on 27 June 2011 by *The Nikki*, Japan's largest business daily newspaper showed that seventy per cent of Japanese people oppose the restarting of the reactors, despite the prospect of black-outs. In a similar poll on 14 June 2011, for the daily newspaper, *Asahi Shimbun*, seventy-four per cent of respondents said they supported a policy that would phase out nuclear power and eventually abandon it altogether.

Abandoning Nuclear Power will not be Easy

Writing in *The New York Times* on 30 May 2011, reporters Martin Fackler and Norimitsu Onishi give numerous examples of how difficult it will be for rural communities in Japan, which have benefited enormously from subsidies associated with the nuclear industry, to abandon nuclear power.[36] The authors describe how the people of Kasima (a rural area of Japan), especially the local fishermen, mounted a massive campaign to stop the construction of the Shimane nuclear plant in the early 1970s. Twenty years later, when the Chugoku Electric company planned to build another reactor on the site, the local people, including the fishing cooperative, mounted a vigorous campaign, this time in favour of building the reactor. There are two main reasons for this remarkable U-turn. Firstly, the Japanese government gives enormous subsidies to communities which accept nuclear power plants. In Kashima, the government built the Fukada Sports Park. The facilities include a baseball diamond, floodlit tennis courts, a soccer field and a $35 million gymnasium with an indoor swimming pool and an Olympic-size volleyball area.

The second reason for the U-turn is that the rural communities, which are willing to host nuclear power plants are now almost completely dependent economically on the nuclear industry in their

---

36. Martin Fackler and Norikitsu Onishi, 'In Japan, A Culture That Promotes Nuclear Dependency,' *The New York Times*, 30 May 2011, http://www.nytimes.com /2011/05/31/world/asia/31japan.html.

area. Traditionally, these communities depended on a thriving fishing industry and farming. But these occupations have declined dramatically in the past forty years. The journalists interviewed a sixty-three-year-old fisherman called Tsuneyoshi Adachi. He admits that he was active in the campaign against building the nuclear plants in the 1970s and in the early 1980s. However, once the compensation payments began to flow into the communities, people who had opposed the building of the reactors were often ostracised by their neighbours. The peer-pressure to desist from campaigning was so strong in that tightly-knit community that Mr Adachi was unwilling to oppose the building of the third reactor in the 1990s. Many rural areas and small towns are now totally dependent on the revenue from the nuclear industry. According to Shuji Shimizu, a professor of public finance at Fukushima University,' this structure of dependency makes it impossible for communities to speak out against the plant or nuclear power.'[37]

The source of the money for these subsidies is a tax which is levied on each energy customer. This was introduced by Prime Minister Kakuei Tanaka in 1974. In many communities, the impact of the first subsidy began to dwindle as the first nuclear reactor aged and faced shutdown. Many communities then opted for a second reactor or a third one to keep the subsidies flowing into the community. According to Daniel Aldrich, a political scientist at Purdue University, who has written about how communities become dependent on the wages and spending power of nuclear power plants: 'The local community gets used to the spending power they got for the first reactor – and the second, third, fourth and fifth reactors help them keep up (their standard of living).'[38] This is why many small towns and rural areas which benefited from generous state subsidies are worried by Prime Minister Kan's statement about not building any more nuclear power plants in Japan.

On 10 June 2011, approximately 20,000 people attended rallies against the use of nuclear power in Tokyo and other cities. There has been growing anger in Japan at the manner in which the government handled the accident at Fukushima, particularly

37. Ibid.
38. Ibid.

since it became clear that the release of radioactive material was far worse than previously thought. Parents are worried about the health of their children. Fishermen and farmers are angry about the damage to their livelihoods. The disaster has prompted a nationwide debate about Japan's heavy reliance on nuclear power, despite the country's history of devastating earthquakes and tsunamis. 'We now know the dangers of relying on nuclear power, and it's time to make a change.' This is what Hajime Matsumoto, one of the rally's organisers, told a crowd that eventually grew to about 20,000 in a square in central Tokyo.[39]

Those who organised the rallies in Tokyo and in other places around the country say that the demonstration was remarkable not because of its size, but because it happened at all in a country that places a high value on conformity and order. 'The Japanese haven't been big protesters, at least until recently,' said Junichi Sato, programme director of the environmental group Greenpeace Japan, who said he had organised enough poorly-attended rallies to know. 'They're taking the first steps toward making themselves heard.'[40] For many of those who attended the rallies, it was the first time they have come out on the streets to protest against any government policy.

On 3 August 2011, the Japanese parliament passed a law which will allow public funds to be used to bolster the company which is operating the crippled Fukushima Daiichi nuclear plant and to help pay damages which will amount to billions of dollars in compensation claims.[41] The law creates a state-backed fund that will pay damages to victims of the disaster at the Fukushima nuclear power plant. The government will pay nearly $26 billion into the fund, Banri Kaieda, the Trade Minister, told lawmakers on the Tuesday following the disaster.

Analysts believe that swift compensation payments are vital, not only in helping victims recover from the disaster, but also in helping to kick-start the local economy. Analysts also recognise that the size of the payments could make Tepco insolvent.

---

39. Hiroko Tabuchi, *The New York Times*, 11 June 2010, http://www.nytimes.com/2011/06/12/world/asia/12japan.html.
40. Ibid.
41. Hiroko Tabuchi, Japanese Prime Minister says governemt shares blame for nuclear disaster,' *The New York Times*, 3 March 2012.

Mr Yoshihiko succeeded Prime Minister Naoto Kan in September 2011. He seemed to renege on his predecessor's pledge to phase out nuclear energy in Japan. In a statement released the week before the first anniversary of the disaster at the Fukushima Daiichi nuclear power plant, he acknowledged that 'officials had been blinded by a false belief in the country's technological infallibility.' The government, the operators and the academic world were all too steeped in a safety myth. 'Everybody must share the pain of responsibility.'[42] But, in the same statement, he indicated that he was intent on restarting some of the country's nuclear power reactors. It remains to be seen whether he will be able to convince a public who had become very sceptical about politicians and so-called nuclear experts.

Officials at the Fukushima Nuclear Power Plant were Fired
Reuters reported that, in another effort to restore confidence, the Japanese government also fired three senior bureaucrats who were in charge of nuclear power policy, holding them to account for a series of scandals over the government's relationship with the power industry. The officials were Kazuo Matsunaga, the top bureaucrat at the Trade Ministry, Nobuaki Terasaka, chief of the Nuclear and Industrial Safety Agency, and Tetsuhiro Hosono, leader of the Agency for Natural Resources and Energy.[43]

One significant development took place at the annual commemoration of the dropping of the atomic bomb on Hiroshima on 6 August 1945. Many of the survivors of that terrible ordeal have begun to voice their opposition to civilian nuclear power as well. Writing in *The New York Times* on 6 August 2011, Martin Fackler describes the reaction of Masahito Hirose, who in 1945 saw the mushroom cloud rise high above Nagasaki, after the atom bomb had been dropped. He quietly accepted Japan's postwar embrace of nuclear-generated power, believing government assurances that it was both safe and necessary for the nation's economic rise. That, however, was before the 11 March 2011 disaster at the

---

42. Hiroko Tabuchi, 3 August 2011, 'Japan Passes Law Supporting Stricken Nuclear Plant's Operator,' http://www.nytimes.com/2011/08/04/world/asia/04japan.html.
43. Ibid.

Fukushima Daiichi nuclear plant in northern Japan. Masahito Hirose was aghast at the catastrophic failure of nuclear technology, and outraged by revelations that the government and the power industry had planted pro-nuclear activists at town hall-style meetings. He believed that elderly atomic bomb survivors, even though they are dwindling in numbers, now have an obligation to oppose civilian nuclear power as well as nuclear weapons.[44]

As both Hiroshima and Nagasaki observed the 66th anniversary of the American atomic attacks at the end of the Second World War, the survivors hoped that they could use their unique moral standing, as the only victims of nuclear bombings, to wean both Japan and the world from what they see as humankind's tragedy-prone efforts to tap the atom. 'Is it Japan's fate to repeatedly serve as a warning to the world about the dangers of radiation?' said Mr Hirose, aged eighty-one, who was a junior high school student when an American bomb obliterated much of Nagasaki, killing about 40,000 people instantly. 'I wish we had found the courage to speak out earlier against nuclear power,' he said.[45]

On 6 May 2011, the Japanese Prime Minister, Naoto Kan, requested the closure of the Hamaoka nuclear power plant which is located about 120 miles south-west of Tokyo, until it could build stronger defences against earthquakes and tsunamis. He had faced withering criticism for the way he handled the crisis at the Fukushima Daiichi plant, which probably accounted for the fact that he has moved rather quickly, in Japanese terms, against the Hamaoka Nuclear Plant.

Concerns about the safety of the Hamaoka reactors have previously been raised. In 2009, the operator, Chubu Electric Power Company, opted to decommission two of the oldest reactors on the site, rather than upgrading them to withstand earthquakes and tsunamis. These two reactors were built in the 1970s. The company had hoped that the three reactors, built in the 1980s, which they are now being asked to shut down could have withstood

44. Martin Fackler, 'Atomic Bomb Survivors Join Nuclear Opposition,' *The New York Times*, 6 August 2011.
http://www.nytimes.com/2011/08/07/world/asia/07hiroshima.html.
45. Ibid.

strong earthquakes. Closing the three Hamaoka reactors, with a generating capacity of 3,500 megawatts, the equivalent of seven per cent of Japan's nuclear generating capacity, will have a huge impact on Japanese life and, especially, business.

Not everyone in Japan is happy at merely shutting down nuclear reactors. Katsuhiko Ishibashi, a seismologist at Kobe University, who has consistently argued for more stringent regulation of the nuclear industry, points out that the plants will remain vulnerable to both earthquakes and tsunamis as they cool down. He argues for immediate action to protect the plants.[46]

Other nuclear power plants in Japan are also causing concern. The Kashiwazaki-Kariwa nuclear power plant on the coast of the Sea of Japan was damaged by an earthquake of 6.6 magnitude on the Richter scale in 2007. The quake caused a fire which was quickly extinguished. The plant was shut down for two years in order to undergo repairs and government inspection. Four of the seven reactors have now been restarted.[47]

One of the reasons why people are concerned about the safety of nuclear power plants is because they do not believe what they have been told and they feel there is a lack of transparency. For example, no journalists were allowed to visit the crippled reactors at Fukushima from the time the earthquake and tsunami took place on 11 March 2011 until the weekend of 12 November 2011. On 11 November 2011, thirty-six journalists, wearing protective suits, double gloves, double layers of plastic booties over their shoes, hair covering and respirator masks, were driven around the stricken plant. As the group approached the plant, radiation readings rose to 0.7 microsieverts (mSv) per hour. The levels began rising as they came closer to the plant. One of the first things which the journalists passed were large tanks full of contaminated water. Tepco estimates that 90,000 tonnes of water are stored in these tanks. Next, they saw a cluster of large white tents surrounded by black sand bags. This is where the reactors were housed. The first reactor was covered by a new superstructure. The second reactor was intact, while the third had collapsed into a pile of rubble.

46. Ibid.
47. Ibid.

Cranes and bulldozers were still clearing up the mess seven months after the disaster. Reactor number 4 was also severely damaged as the entire south side had been blown out. At about five hundred metres from the crippled reactors, the microsieverts reading touched 50ms per hour. At the base of each reactor, this had increased dramatically to 1,000ms per hour. The power of the tsunami was evident at the base of the reactor building. It was filled with debris, warped metal, cars and trucks which had been thrown into pools together.

When the journalists entered the safety centre, they were asked to remove their boots. In the next room, their protective gear was removed by workers using scissors. Gloves and masks were also removed. They were briefed by Tetsuya Terasawa, a spokesman for Tepco. He told them that the temperature at the three damaged reactors was now below 100°C. He conceded that there was 40,000 tonnes of water at the bottom of the reactor buildings, which could not be drained because more water would flow in. Tepco is still pouring cold water on the three damaged reactors to bring them to what is called 'cold shutdown'.[48] Recently, Tepco were forced to admit that if they stopped dousing the reactors with cooling water, the fuel would heat up and the process of nuclear fission could begin again. The government minister in charge of the nuclear crisis, Goshi Hosono, complimented the workers on the progress which they had made to date, in particular that they were on schedule to achieve cold shutdown before the end of 2011. The bad news is that it will take thirty years to dismantle the crippled reactors.

As of November 2011, eighty per cent of Japan's fifty-four nuclear reactors were offline, either because they were damaged by the earthquake or are facing safety checks. Starting up each one of these reactors will not be easy. There is a pervasive scepticism about the safety of nuclear reactors in a country which is prone to earthquakes and tsunamis.[49]

In January 2012, the Chief Secretary to the Japanese Cabinet, Osamu Fujimura, revealed that there was a loophole in the law which allowed for the closure of existing nuclear power plants

---

48. See p. 22 of this book for an explanation of 'cold shutdown'.
49. David McNeill, 'Entering Japan's nuclear wasteland,' *The Irish Times*, 15 November 2011, p. 9.

which have been in operation for forty years or more. He told reporters that nuclear power plants will be allowed to operate for a further twenty years, if they meet very stringent safety standards.[50] According to the Japanese Ministry of Trade, thirteen nuclear reactors will reach the forty-year mark by 2020. If this pushes through, it would mean that Japan would not be free of nuclear power plants until 2069.[51]

The most positive news about the nuclear accident at the Fukushima Daiichi nuclear power plant came on 15 January 2012, when it was announced that an independent panel of specialists have been appointed to review and, if necessary, challenge the Japanese government's account of the accident. One of the main focal points of their investigation will be to establish how much damage was done to the reactors before the tsunami hit the plant.[52] The investigating team will have the power to subpoena witnesses. The chair of the panel is Kiyoshi Kurokawa, who is a former leader of Tokyo University's medical department. One of the team members is the Nobel laureate, Koichi Taaka. Mr Kurokawa said that the panel would investigate the issues thoroughly and that there will be no untouchable, sacred cows.[53] According to Mr Kurokawa, 'For Japan to regain global credibility, we need an investigation into the disaster that is completely independent.'[54]

In an article in *The New York Times*, Hiroko Tabuchi describes the confused and haphazard way that has characterised the efforts to clean-up the contamination area around the stricken reactors at Fukushima Daiichi nuclear power plant. The village of Litate located about twenty miles from the ravaged nuclear plant had a population of 6,500 before March 2011. Five hundred workers were involved in the clean-up operation. Each worker wore a hazmat suit, which is an impermeable garment that covers the

50. Hiroko Tabuchi, 'Japanese Reactors Could Operate Beyond 40-Year Cap,' *The New York Times*, 19 January 2012, http://www.nytimes.com/2012/01/19/world/asia/japanese-nuclear-reactors-could-operate-beyond-40-year-cap.html.
51. Ibid.
52. Hiroko Tabachi, 'Panel Challenges Japan's Account of Nuclear Disaster,' *The New York Times*, 15 January 2012, http://www.nytimes.com/2012/01/16/business/global/independent-panel-to-start-inquiry-into-japans-nuclear-crisis.html.
53. Ibid.
54. Ibid.

whole body and provides protection from hazardous materials. They also wore respirator masks. 'Dig five centimetres or ten centimetres deep here,' a site supervisor asked his colleagues, pointing to a patch of radioactive topsoil to be removed. He then gestured across the village square toward the community centre. 'Isn't that going to be demolished? Shall we decontaminate it or not?'[55] Tabuchi went on to write that a day labourer, who was wiping down the windows of the local school, shrugged his shoulders at the haphazard approach of the decontamination team. This man said, 'we are all amateurs, nobody really knows how to clean-up radiation.'[56] Lack of competence has not deterred the Japanese government from awarding lucrative contracts to rehabilitate the contaminated area of 8,000 square miles which is about the size of New Jersey in the US.

Furthermore, many people are critical of the fact that the government is handing out these contracts to large building contractors who have no particular expertise in cleaning up sites which have been contaminated with nuclear elements. These companies benefited hugely from the Japanese government's embrace of nuclear energy in the first place. Three companies helped build forty-five of Japan's fifty-four nuclear plants, including the Fukushima Daiichi plant. Kiyoshi Sakurai, who worked at what was the forerunner company to the Japan Atomic Energy Agency and is a vocal critic of the nuclear industry, believes that the clean-up operation is 'a scam. Decontamination is becoming big business. The Japanese nuclear industry is run so that the more you fail, the more money you receive.'[57] Once again, there is an unhealthily cosy relationship between the nuclear industry, large corporations and the Japanese government.

Former Prime Minister Naoto Kan Criticizes Nuclear Power
On 27 May 2012, the former prime minister of Japan, Naoto Kan, told a parliamentary inquiry into the Fukushima accident, and the

55. Hiroko Tabuchi, 'A Confused Nuclear Cleanup,' *The New York Times*, 10 February 2012, http://www.nytimes.com/2012/02/11/business/global/after-fukushima-diaster-a-confused-effort-at-cleanup.html.
56. Ibid.
57. Ibid.

events that followed it, that Japan should discard nuclear power because it is too dangerous. He told the inquiry that the politically-powerful nuclear industry was trying to push Japan back into restarting its nuclear reactors. He reiterated that the safety procedures at Japan's nuclear power plants were inadequate because the country's energy policy had been hijacked by what he called the 'nuclear village'.[58] This is the term used to refer to the fact that the energy companies, the regulators and the researchers have worked closely together to promote the nuclear industry.

Naoto Kan complained that the nuclear regulators and the plant's operator, Tokyo Electric Power (Tepco), had kept him in the dark about crucial details in the immediate aftermath of the 11 March 2011 earthquake and subsequent tsunami, which knocked out the back-up cooling system, causing three of the plant's reactors to meltdown. He recalled the most extraordinary moment of the crisis, when he stormed into Tepco's headquarters in Tokyo and demanded that Tepco staff remain at the stricken Fukushima plant. The company had planned to evacuate the staff. He said that he was willing to put his own life in danger in order to prevent the disaster from getting much worse. He feared that additional meltdowns could 'release into the air and sea many times, no, many dozens of times, many hundreds of times the radiation released by Chernobyl'.[59] He said that the prospect of losing Tokyo made him realise that nuclear power was too risky. According to him, 'It is impossible to ensure safety sufficiently to prevent the risk of a national collapse. Experiencing the accident convinced me that the best way to make nuclear plants safe was not to rely on them, but rather to get rid of them.'[60] Mr Kan also used his testimony to the parliamentary inquiry to criticise the relatively pro-nuclear stance of his successor, Mr Yoshihiko, who replaced him in September 2011.

---

58. Martin Fackler, 'Japan's Former Leader Condemns Nuclear Power,' *The New York Times*, 28 May 2012. http://www.nytimes.com/2012/05/29/world/asia/japans-naoto-kan-condemns-nuclear-power.html.
59. Ibid.
60. Ibid.

Japanese Government Gives Permission to Restart Nuclear Reactors.
Prime Minister Yoshihiko Noda did not take his predecessor's
advice. He appeared on television on 8 June 2012 and argued that
it was important to restart nuclear power plants in June 2012
so that there would be sufficient electric power during the hot
summer of 2012. He defended his government's decision made on
9 May 2012 to give permission to the Kansai Electric Power Co. in
Ohi in Western Japan to restart two nuclear reactors. The government claimed that the nuclear power plants had undergone extensive maintenance and safety checks.

He maintained that, with nuclear power plants idle, the high
cost of energy, especially electricity, was making Japanese indus-
tries uncompetitive. As a result, many businesses were threatening
to relocate overseas to China or South east Asia. Business leaders
had been calling for the resumption of nuclear energy.[61] The
Minister for Trade, Yukio Edano, who also holds the energy
portfolio, said that the Japanese government's plans to reduce
Japan's dependence on nuclear power in the medium and long-
term are still on course.

This decision was seen as a clear sign that the lobbying power
of the nuclear power industry is still very strong, despite the huge
public concern for safety in the wake of the Fukushima disaster.
Minister Yukio Edano tried to assuage anxieties by saying that
'based on what we learned from the Fukushima accident, those
measures that need to be taken urgently have been addressed, and
the level of safety has been considerably enhanced (at the Ohi
plant).'[62] The Japanese government, under Prime Minister Noda,
would like to see many nuclear power stations restarted within
one or two years. High on the restarting list is the 890 megawatt
No. 3 reactor at Ikata in southern Japan. The Nuclear and Industry
Safety Agency, which was the old watchdog on the nuclear industry, has approved stress tests on this reactor. Next in line for
restarting are two reactors owned by Kokkaido Electric Power

61. Reuters, 'Japan Approves Two Reactor Restarts, More Seen Ahead,' *The New
York Times*, June 16th 2012. http://www.nytimes.com/reuters/2012/06/16/
world/asia/16reuters-japan-nuclear.html.
62. Ibid.

and located in Tomari in northern Japan and two more owned by
the same company in Shika on the western coast of Japan.

Despite the prime minister's direct appeal, a poll showed that
most Japanese people were opposed to restarting the reactors.
Opponents point out that the new earthquake-resistant control
centre and other safety measures at Ohi will not be completed for
years. Before the Prime Minister's TV appearance, 10,000
protestors convened outside the Prime Minister's office to regis-
ter their opposition to restarting nuclear reactors. Though there
was a strong police presence, the demonstrators shouted, 'lives
matter more than the economy'. Civil Society Organisations
(CSOs) accused the prime minister of exposing the Japanese
environment and the Japanese people to needless health risks.[63]
Anti-nuclear activists have collected more than 7.5 million signa-
tures on a petition calling for the end of nuclear power in Japan.
Among those who signed was the celebrated author Kenzaburo
Oe who was awarded the Nobel Prize in Literature 1994.

Mitsuru Obe and Chester Dawson writing in the Wall Street
Journal detected an ambivalence, even in the area around Ohi,
towards restarting the reactors. The mayor of the town says he is
happy with the precautions which have been taken at the power
plant. Forty miles away, in the city of Nagahama, people were
opposed to restarting the nuclear reactors at all.[64] They claim that
proper evacuation procedures have not been put in place in case
there was another Fukushima-like accident.

Critics of nuclear power also point to the delay in setting up
a competent and independent nuclear regulatory agency. The
former regulatory agency was much too close to Tokyo Electric
Power Company (Tepco) the company that operated the
Fukushima Daiichi reactors. This mistrust of both the nuclear
industry and the regulatory agency is still evident. For many
Japanese, the scale of the accident at Fukushima Daiichi and the
poor response from the government and the regulatory agency

63. Ibid.
64. Mitsuru Obe and Chester Dawson, The Wall Street Journal, 18 June 2012,
'Nuclear-Restart Plans Divide Japan', http://online.wsj.com/article/SB1000
1424052702303444204577460272545747302.html.

has destroyed the public's belief in the 'safety of nuclear power myth' which the industry has promoted for five decades. On 7 June 2012, the Japanese Parliament had approved legislation designed to create a new regulatory agency. The problem is that it will take months to get this agency up and running.

In Tokyo, Thousands Protest at the Restarting of a Nuclear Power Plant
On 28 June 2012, tens of thousands of demonstrators gathered in front of the Japanese prime minister's residence to protest at the decision to restart a nuclear power plant. The crowd, which included women, children and men in suits, chanted the slogan, 'No more Fukushimas.' The organisers claimed that 150,000 people took part in the demonstrations. The police put the number at a mere 17,000, whereas the local media estimated the crowd at between 20,000 and 45,000. Regardless of the precise number, it was the largest protest in central Tokyo since the 1960s.[65]

Report finds Fukushima Plant Meltdown 'Made in Japan'
A 641-page report released on 5 July 2012 challenged the government's and industry's version of events which led to the disaster at Fukushima. The report was the work of the Fukushima Nuclear Accident Independent Investigation Commission which was set up in the wake of the meltdown at the Fukushima Daiichi nuclear power stations. The chairman, Dr Kiyoshi Kurokawa, a medical doctor and emeritus professor at Tokyo University, found that the meltdown was a product of 'a multitude of errors and willful negligence' by the government, safety officials and the plant's operator Tepco.[66] Dr Kurokawa considers that the blunders were also due to central traits in Japanese culture. One of these traits is the reluctance to question authority. Because of the collusion between the government, the nuclear regulators and Tepco, the

65. Martin Fackler, 'In Tokyo, Thousands Protest the Restarting of a Nuclear Power Plant,' *The New York Times*, 29 June 2012, http://www.nytimes.com /2012/06/30/world/asia/thousands-in-tokyo-protest-the-restarting-of-a-nuclear-plant.html.
66. Justin McCurry, 'Fukushima plant meltdown "made in Japan",' *The Guardian*, 6 July 2012, p. 21.

authors have come to the conclusion that the accident was clearly 'man-made'. Interestingly, the report challenges the sequence of events as presented by Tepco and the Japanese government. The company claims that the meltdown at Reactor 1 happened after the 14-metre-high tsunami had destroyed the back-up diesel generators which were designed to keep coolants flowing to the reactor when electric power failed for any reason. This report believes that the earthquake, registering 9.1 on the Richter scale, could have burst the pipes even before tsunami hit the plant.[67] This finding will be seized upon by the anti-nuclear lobby which argues that all nuclear power plants are unsafe because Japan is prone to severe earthquakes and tsunamis.

The report contradicts the then Prime Minister Naoto Kan's account of what happened. He has portrayed himself as a decisive leader who was willing to challenge top officials in Tepco whom he claimed had ordered an evacuation of all Tepco personnel from the stricken plant. The report states that there was no evidence that the operator planned to abandon the plant and, furthermore, that meddling from Mr Kan and his high-profile visit to the nuclear power station on the day after the accident in fact confused the initial response. The prime minister's visit 'diverted the attention and time of the on-site operational staff and confused the line of command'.[68]

The report is very critical of the top management at Tepco. It claims that the Tepco president, Masataka Shimizu failed to report clearly to the prime minister's office what was actually happening and to give a clear idea of how the company planned to deal with the accident. This, in turn, led to a breakdown of trust between the company and the government.

The report goes on to accuse Tepco, the regulators and the Nuclear Safety Commission of failing to take adequate safety measures, for the Fukushima nuclear power plant which was built in an area susceptible to powerful earthquakes, followed by

---

67. Ibid.
68. Hiroko Tabuchi, 'Inquiry Declares Fukushima Crisis a Man-Made Disaster,' *The New York Times*, 5 July 2012, http://www.nytimes.com/2012/07/06/world/asia/fukushima-nuclear-crisis-a-man-made-disaster-report-says.html.

tsunamis. In 2006, the Japanese Nuclear Safety Commission revised earthquake resistance standards in, and ordered nuclear operators to inspect, their reactors in the light of the new regulations. The report found that Tepco did not carry out these instructions. Neither did the Nuclear Safety Commission check whether the nuclear operators were in compliance with these new standards.

The authors state, 'We believe that the root causes were the organizational and regulatory system that supported faulty rationales for decisions and actions, rather than issues relating to the competence of any specific individual. Across the board the commission found ignorance and arrogance unforgiveable for anyone or any organization that deals with nuclear power.'[69]

---

69. Ibid.

CHAPTER THREE

The Impact of Fukushima on Other Countries

China

Within a few days of the earthquake and tsunami which happened near the city of Sendai, situated off the north-east coast of Japan, China's State Council suspended its approval of the construction of nuclear plants which had been planned for many places across its sprawling country. In August 2011, the Chinese government decided to resume its ambitious programme of building nuclear reactors. By 2020, China plans to build between fifty and sixty more nuclear power stations. This is more than all the rest of the world put together.

The really worrying aspect about China's nuclear programme is that it is opting for a nuclear technology which many consider to be a questionable technology. According to a US cable released by WikiLeaks, the Chinese are planning to build their own reactors, called CPR-1000, based on an old technology pioneered by the US power corporation, Westinghouse. The cable claims that by the time these reactors have reached the end of their use, their technology will be one hundred years old. The leaked cable stated that 'by bypassing the passive safety technology of the AP1000 which, according to Westinghouse, is one hundred times safer than the CPR-1000, China is vastly increasing the aggregate risk of its nuclear power fleet.'[1] The new passive technology is meant to ensure that reactors shut down automatically in the event of a disaster, without having to wait for human intervention, which may not be readily available, as was seen at Fukushima.

China's plans to build multiple nuclear power stations is very worrying in the light of the fact that seismic activity is common across China. On 12 May 2008, an earthquake of magnitude 8 on the Richter scale hit the Sichuan province. It is estimated that it killed at least 68,000 people. The epicentre was eighty kilometres north-west of Chengdu, the capital of Sichuan province.

---

1. Jonathan Watts, 'China's cheap nuclear plants "increase risk",' *The Guardian*, 26 August 2011, p. 25.

The earthquake was felt as far away as Beijing, which is 1,500 kilometres away, and even in Shanghai, which is 1,700 kilometres from the epicentre, office buildings swayed with the tremor.

The earthquake in Tangshan in 1976, which registered 8.2 on the Richter scale destroyed eighty-nine per cent of homes and seventy-eight per cent of all factories. According to Chinese records, 240,000 people lost their lives. International observers put the number of dead at around 750,000. In the wake of that earthquake, China introduced stringent building regulations. But the collapse of schools, hospitals and factories across Sichuan, as a result of the 2008 earthquake raised serious questions about whether the building regulations are being strictly enforced. In a society where political control is still very prevalent, it is conceivable that, through political pressure, corners could also be cut in the rush to build so many nuclear power generating plants. The Chinese government refused to give details of the number of students who died because schools and dormitories collapsed as a result of the earthquake in the Sichuan province. Another cause for concern was the reports that emerged in July 2008, that the authorities were conducting a campaign to buy the silence of those parents who lost sons and daughters as a result of the quake. It appears that many parents were given a payment of $8,000 and the promise of a pension in exchange for remaining silent about the deaths of their children.

On 23 January 1556, the most devastating earthquake in recorded history took place in China. Ninety-seven counties in the provinces of Shaanxi, Shanxi, Henan, Gansu, Hebei, Shandong, Hubei, Hunan, Jiangsu and Anhui were affected. It is estimated that approximately 830,000 people lost their lives.

In light of the above, it should come as no surprise that not everyone in China is happy with this headlong rush to build nuclear power plants. In 2011, He Zuoxiu, the scientist who developed China's first atomic bomb, said that China's plan to increase the production of nuclear energy twenty-fold by 2030, could be as disastrous as Mao Zedong's Great Leap Forward in the 1950s. That experiment to jump-start industrialisation in China cost millions of lives. Writing in *Science Times*, He Zuoxiu asked, 'Are we really ready for this kind of giddy speed [of nuclear power development]? I think not – we're seriously under-prepared, especially on the safety front.'[2]

People in the nuclear industry are also worried. Gavin Lu, a Westinghouse representative, was quoted in one of the leaked cables as saying, 'The biggest potential bottleneck is human resources – coming up with enough trained personnel to build and operate all these new plants, as well as regulate the industry.'[3]

Germany

Even before the Chinese had shown their hand, the German chancellor, Angela Merkel, moved to close seven of that country's seventeen nuclear power stations. During the 2009 election, Angela Merkel promised to phase out nuclear power stations over a period of twenty years. After the election, she reneged on her commitment by trying to extend the life of the nuclear reactors in the country for between ten and twenty years. Her party, the Christian Democratic Union (CDU), paid dearly for this decision. The CDU lost the state election in Baden-Württemberg. The CDU had held this state since 1953. The Green Party was opposed to nuclear power and, as a result, increased its vote to twenty-five per cent. It is now in negotiations with the Social Democrats (SPD) which, if successful, will result in a Green party member becoming a state premier in Germany for the first time.[4]

A committee, appointed by Chancellor Angela Merkel, in the aftermath of the Fukushima accident and drawn from the energy industry and non-government organisations, recommended that Germany should close all its nuclear power plants by the year 2021 and that the country should rely on other forms of energy.[5] In 2011, nuclear power was responsible for 22.6 per cent of Germany's electricity. Nuclear power in Germany is generated by seventeen reactors. Six are boiling water reactors, similar to the

---

2. Ibid.
3. Ibid.
4. Derek Scally, 'Merkel feels the pain after defeat in election,' *The Irish Times*, 28 March 2011, p. 9.
5. Judy Dempsey, 'Panel Urges Germany to Close Nuclear Plants by 2021,' *The New York Times*, 12 May 2011, p. B7.

reactors at Fukushima and eleven use pressurised water. Forty-two per cent of Germany's electricity comes from coal-fired plants. Natural gas provides for 13.6 per cent, while renewable sources, mainly from wind and solar energy, generate 16.5 per cent. There is a strong anti-nuclear movement in Germany, but the nuclear industry is also powerful. Many of the large companies are warning that the move away from nuclear power will have a disastrous impact on the economy.[6] The Ethics Commission, which produced the review for the chancellor, was led by Klaus Topfer, who is a former environment minister and executive director of the United Nations Environment Programme (UNEP). He refutes the claims from the nuclear industry and argues that, 'a withdrawal from nuclear power will spur growth, offer enormous technical, economic and social opportunities to position Germany even further as an exporter of sustainable products and services.'[7] But whatever the benefits in the future from renewable energy, the committee called for the closing of the seventeen reactors currently in use for safety reasons. It states that 'The withdrawal is necessary to fundamentally eliminate risks.'[8] Environmentalists and other European governments are closely monitoring Germany's move away from nuclear power.

On 30 May 2011, a forty-eight page document on energy security argued that an 'exit from nuclear energy can be achieved within a decade'.[9] The document goes on to make the point that Germany must make a binding commitment to producing energy from non-nuclear sources. 'Only a clearly delineated goal can provide the necessary planning and investment security.'[10] The document also said that 'the exit (from nuclear power) should be designed so as not to endanger the competitiveness of industry and the economy.' The EU Energy Commissioner has said that 'Germany's energy policy will only work if there are improvements at the same

---

6. Ibid.
7. Ibid.
8. Ibid.
9. Judy Dempsey and Jack Ewing, 'In Reversal, Germany to Close Nuclear Plants by 2022', *The New York Times*, 30 May 2011, http://www.nytimes.com/2011/05/31/world/europe/31germany.html.
10. Ibid.

time.'[11] Germany will need a better grid infrastructure, increased storage capacity and major investment in renewable energy.

Even before the decision to phase out nuclear energy, Germany was leading the way in installing renewable sources of energy. The Imperial College physicist, Keith Barnhman, points out that Germany has installed more wind power capacity than the entire UK nuclear capacity. In 2009, Germany installed solar photovoltaic systems with a capacity equivalent to approximately four nuclear reactors.[12]

The real bombshell as regards nuclear energy was dropped by Siemens, the giant power company, on 18 September 2011. The Siemens' CEO, Peter Löscher, told the weekly *Der Spiegel* that his company 'will no longer be involved in the overall managing or building or financing of nuclear plants. This chapter is closed for us'.[13] He went on to say that, 'we (Siemens) will from now on supply only conventional equipment such as steam turbines. This means we are restricting ourselves to technologies that are not only for nuclear purposes but can also be used in gas and coal plants.'[14] This is an extraordinary change for a company which has been at the forefront of nuclear power for sixty years. Siemens helped to build all of Germany's nuclear power stations. As recently as 2009, Siemens announced that the company, in collaboration with a Russian company, planned to build up to four hundred nuclear plants by 2030.[15]

Siemens gave two reasons for pulling out of nuclear power plants. The first was the decision of the German government to phase out nuclear power plants by 2020. The second reason was the Fukushima disaster. The decision will cost the company dearly. It will have to pay fines to be allowed to withdraw from a contract with Russia's ROSATOM to build a new nuclear power plant. It

11. Helen Pidd, 'Merkel makes move amid mass anti-nuclear protests,' *The Guardian*, 31 May 2011, p. 17.
12. Paul Dorfman, 'Who to trust on nuclear,' *The Guardian*, 14 April 2011, p. 27.
13. 'Siemens Rocks World With Complete Closure of Nuclear Business', 19 September 2011, http://houseoffoust.com/group/?p=3144.
14. Ibid.
15. Response to Fukushima Siemens to Exit Nuclear Energy Business, www.peopleunlikeus.com/?p=14311, PEOPLEUNLIKEUS, 19 September 2011.

will also have to pay a considerable amount of money to Areva for ending a nuclear contract with that company. Areva is a French public multinational industrial conglomerate, headquartered in the Tour Areva in Courbevoie, Paris. It is mainly associated with nuclear power but it also has interests in other energy projects.

The good news is that Siemens will put a lot of money and research into developing alternative sources of energy. Peter Löscher said that his company aimed to be at the forefront of Germany's ambitious goal to generate thirty-five per cent of its energy from renewable sources by the year 2020.[16]

The Frankfurt-based German state-owned bank KfW – originally known as Kreditanstalt fur Wiederaufbau, which means Reconstruction Credit Institute – estimates that the move away from nuclear energy to renewable sources will cost something in the region of €250 billion between 2011 and 2020. KfW predicts that renewable energy will account for eighty per cent of the total electric power by 2050. In 2011, renewable energy only accounted for fifteen per cent.[17]

Not everyone thinks that Germany's decision to abandon nuclear power is a good thing. Writing in the *NewScientist* in July 2011, David Strahan suggests that the decision was made for political reasons, that it will jeopardise Germany's efforts to reduce greenhouse gases and, finally, that it will make energy prices more expensive for every household in Europe.[18] Around twenty-three per cent of Germany's electricity comes from nuclear power. Germany plans to raise power from renewable sources to thirty-five per cent by 2020. Strahan claims that this will leave a gap of five per cent which will have to be met by building fossil-fuel stations. He maintains that Germany plans to build twenty gigawatts of fossil-fuel power stations by 2020. Trevor Sikorski, head of environmental market research at the London investment bank,

---

16. Derek Scally, 'Siemens exits nuclear energy arena as chief executive says "chapter closed",' *The Irish Times*, 19 September 2011, p. 10, http:// www.nuclear-powerdaily.com/reports/Nuclear_pull-out_to_cost_Germany_250_billion_euros_study_999.html.
17. Staff writer, 'Nuclear pull-out to cost Germany 250 billion euro: study,' *Nuclear Power Daily*, 19 September 2011.
18. David Strahan, 'Nein Danke!' *New Scientist*, 30 July 2011, p. 24.

Barclays Capital, estimates that Germany will emit an extra three hundred million tonnes of carbon dioxide between 2011 and 2020.[19]

Britain

Immediately after the accident at Fukushima, Chris Huhne, the former UK Energy Secretary, asked Mike Weightman, the chief nuclear inspector of the Health and Safety Directorate, to assess the safety record at Britain's nuclear power plants. Huhne acknowledged that Fukushima has changed the nuclear calculus. In an interview with *The Observer*, he conceded that it will now be much more difficult to get private investors to raise enough capital to build the eight new reactors which the government was planning. Huhne told Toby Helm, *The Observer*'s political editor, that 'there are a lot of issues outside the realm of nuclear safety, which we will have to assess. One is what the economics of nuclear power, post Fukushima will be, if there is an increase in the cost of capital for nuclear operators.'[20]

In July 2011, preparatory work on the Hinkley Point nuclear power station was given approval by West Somerset District Council. If it is completed, it will be the first nuclear power plant built in Britain in twenty years. Anti-nuclear campaigners believe that West Somerset District Council has been pressured by the government to approve the site, and villagers, whose lives will be affected, say the project would change the area forever. Crispin Aubrey, of the Stop Hinkley Campaign, argued that the work would leave a 'devastated wasteland' and said it was 'inaccurate' to describe the work which Electricité de France (EDF) has been given permission for, as 'preparatory'. He goes on to say that 'the extent of the activity, the clearance of most vegetation, hedges and trees, the excavation of more than two million cubic metres of soil and rocks, the re-routing of underground streams, the creation of roads and roundabouts, major changes to the landscape ... mean it is effectively the beginning of construction of the proposed Hinkley Point nuclear power station.'[21]

---

19. Ibid.

20. Toby Helm, 'Nuclear might cease to be an option for UK, admits Huhne,' *The Observer*, 20 March 2011, p. 11.

21. Steven Morris, 'Hinkley C nuclear station gets green light for preparatory work,' *The Guardian*, 29 July 2011.

Supporters of nuclear power such as David Rosser, who is the regional director of the Confederation of British Industry, for the South-West and Wales said: 'We believe it critical that we are able to guarantee a secure and low carbon energy mix for the UK in the decades to come.'[22] Others such as Rupert Cox, chief executive director of Somerset Chamber of Commerce, point to the economic benefits of having a nuclear power station in an area. According to Cox: 'It's an opportunity to kick-start the local economy – thousands of jobs during construction, hundreds for the many years of operation and millions of pounds for the local economy and the skills and training provision in Somerset.'[23]

The most dramatic consequence for Britain of the accident at Fukushima is the closing of the controversial Sellafield MOX nuclear fuel plant.[24] There are three ways of dealing with the highly-radioactive plutonium powder that is produced as waste at Thorp reprocessing plant in West Cumbria. The radioactive material can be buried, though there isn't even consensus on a suitable site for this. Secondly, it can be turned into so-called 'mixed oxide' (MOX) fuel for reuse in converted nuclear reactors, or it can be burned in 'fast breed' reactors. According to an editorial in *The Independent*, Britain's MOX programme is also in disarray for a variety of reasons which include cost overruns and the fact that the plant has only produced a fraction of what it claimed it would produce. The final nail in the MOX coffin was the decision of the Japanese government, in the wake of the Fukushima Daiichi disaster, to pull the plug on contracts made with the Sellafield facility.[25]

The editorial stated that 'taken together, Britain's efforts to reprocess its spent nuclear fuel have been characterised by incompetence, bad decisions and ballooning costs. In fairness to the Nuclear Decommissioning Authority (NDA), many of the problems are the legacy of the past. Indeed Chris Huhne – then Energy Secretary – branded the nuclear sector as perhaps the most expensive failure of post-war policy-making. But it is not enough to blame the past. Although the NDA says that Evaporator D can

22. Ibid.
23. Ibid.
24. Ibid.
25. 'Leading article: An unhappy record on reprocessing,' *The Independent*, 14 February 2012.

be used for other purposes after Thorp has closed, that hardly excuses the mistaken specification. Indeed with an ambitious nuclear new-build programme on the cards, Britain cannot afford for the NDA to continue in the mould of its bungling predecessors.'[26]

On 3 August 2011, Tony Fountain, chief executive of the Nuclear Decommissioning Authority (NDA), told workers that, 'the reason for this [closure] is directly related to the tragic events in Japan following the tsunami and its ongoing impact on the power markets. As a consequence, we no longer have a customer for this facility, or funding.'[27] As a result of the closure, six hundred people will lose their jobs.[28] The company said that many could be redeployed in other parts of the Sellafield complex.

Fountain admitted that the plant had suffered 'many years of disappointing performance' that has been funded by the taxpayer. He said the main factors which saved the plant in recent years had been the commitment of Japanese utilities to reusing nuclear fuel, and their support for the UK as a 'centre of excellence'. But, with the crisis in the Japanese nuclear industry, that route is no longer viable.[29] The Japanese Hamaoka plant, owned by Chubu, the intended recipient of the first fuel, is currently closed, awaiting extensive reinforcement work. Speculation about the future of the plant has been rife for months, as it became clear that the Japanese nuclear industry was unlikely to recover after Fukushima.

The NDA said it would continue to store Japanese plutonium safely, and further develop discussions with the Japanese customers on a responsible approach to support the Japanese utilities' policy for the reuse of their material. Many believe that the closure of the Sellafield MOX plant will have a knock-on effect on the troubled Thorp reprocessing plant also. The NDA denied that it was considering closing Thorp, saying the two situations were 'unrelated' and that the business case for Thorp, which produces plutonium from other nuclear waste, continued to be strong.

---

26. Ibid.
27. Ibid.
28. Fiona Harvey, 'Sellafield Mox nuclear fuel plant to close', *The Guardian*, 4 August 2010, http://www.guardian.co.uk/environment/2011/aug/03/sellafield-mox-plant-close/print.
29. Ibid.

However, the Thorp plant was constructed on the same premise as the Sellafield MOX plant, so that there would be a market for reprocessed fuels to be used, in nuclear reactors. That market has proved extremely small – Japan has been the only customer – and the demise of the Japanese nuclear industry has closed down the market altogether. The Thorp plant is being decommissioned at a cost of £6.5 billion. Thorp was always a controversial project. In the year 2000, Ireland and five Nordic countries campaigned unsuccessfully against the opening of the facility. They opposed it also at the United Nations Law of the Sea Tribunal because of its possible pollution of the oceans. They also pointed out that it could become a target for terrorists. All of these representations were rebuffed by the British government. In 2004, there was a major spill of radioactive material at Thorp. Luckily, it was contained within the facility and did not present a threat to people or the environment. Later, a much larger leakage of radioactive material which had gone on for nine months, was discovered. An official inquiry found that there was a complacent managerial and safety culture at Thorp. A fine of a half a million pounds was imposed for breaches of health and safety laws.[30]

The British government knows that the new nuclear plants which they are planning to build with private operators such as France's EDF or Germany's RWE will not use MOX or plutonium. RWE is a German-owned utility company. The government's suggestion that another reactor could be built in the UK that would use MOX as fuel was greeted with extreme scepticism by nuclear industry experts. They said any replacement of the MOX processing plant would be 'another white elephant' that would cost the UK taxpayer billions of pounds as there is little or no market for its products.

Industry experts noted, however, that the government has an interest in continuing to insist that MOX is still viable. If ministers admitted that MOX was not viable, the government would be forced to acknowledge that the hundreds of millions of pounds worth of plutonium that is stored there would have to be recognised as a liability on government balance sheets. However, the pretence

30. Editorial, 'Plant closure at Sellafield,' *The Irish Times*, 9 August 2011, p. 13.

that another MOX plant may be built, allows the plutonium to be reckoned a zero-value asset. Labour MP, Jamie Reed, whose Copeland constituency includes Sellafield, called on the government to lay out details of a potential plan to build a new MOX plant at the site. He said: 'It is now absolutely essential that the new MOX plant is brought forward as quickly as possible. The market for MOX fuel exists and is growing, our plutonium disposition strategy relies upon such a facility and the industry requires it.'[31] He warned that 'gleeful vultures' would seize upon the decision to close the plant and argue against the 'critical national need for a new MOX plant'.[32]

In a far-reaching indictment, the spokeswoman for Greenpeace, Louise Hutchins, said that this scandalous collusion between the British government and the nuclear industry 'highlights the government's blind obsession with nuclear power and shows that neither they nor the industry can be trusted when it comes to nuclear'.[33] A review of the eighty emails sent out from the Department of Energy and Climate Change (DECC) makes it clear that the government officials were more concerned about the fact that the Fukushima accident was undermining public support for the government's nuclear programme, than informing the public about the accident at Fukushima.[34] The British government contacted nuclear power corporations such as EDF Energy, Areva and Westinghouse with a view to drawing up a coordinated public relations strategy to play down the nuclear accident at Fukushima Daiichi.

This was a major setback for the British government's pro-nuclear policy in October 2011 when RWE, the German utility company, indicated that it may abandon its UK nuclear programme. The company is now in the process of reviewing whether it will take part in the construction of two nuclear power plants, one at Wylfa in Wales and the other at Oldbury in

31. Ibid.
32. Ibid.
33. Rob Edwards, 'Revealed: British government's plan to play down Fukushima,' *The Guardian*, 30 June 2011. http://www.guardian.co.uk/environment/2011/jun/30/british-government-plan-play-down-fukushima/print.
34. Ibid.

Gloucestershire.[35] This follows the decision of another utility company, Scottish and Southern Energy (SSE), to withdraw from a nuclear construction programme in Cumbria.

A poll conducted by GlobeScan for the BBC showed that there has been a marked increase, both in those who are opposed to building nuclear power plants and those supporting the development of renewable sources of energy. Twenty-two per cent of the sample agreed that 'nuclear power is relatively safe and an important source of electricity, and we should build more nuclear power plants'. In contrast, seventy-one per cent thought their country 'could almost entirely replace coal and nuclear energy within twenty years by becoming highly energy-efficient and focusing on generating energy from sun and wind'.[36] Globally, thirty-nine per cent of those polled want to continue using existing reactors without building new ones, while thirty per cent would like to shut down all nuclear power plants. In Germany, the opposition to nuclear power grew from seventy-three to ninety per cent. Even in France, the opposition to nuclear power has grown from sixty-one to eighty-three per cent.[37]

Switzerland

In 2008, Switzerland had four nuclear power plants with five nuclear reactors in operation. Nuclear energy was responsible for producing 26.3 TWh, roughly 39.9 per cent of the total electricity produced. The rest came from hydroelectric power stations responsible for 65.9 per cent of electricity. The remaining 4.9 per cent was produced from conventional thermal power plants and other renewable energy sources. Switzerland suspended approvals for three new nuclear reactors and pledged to review safety at all its nuclear installations. On 25 May 2011, the Swiss Cabinet called for the phasing out and decommissioning of the

35. Terry Macalister and Severin Carrell, 'Second firm could abandon UK nuclear building programme,' *The Guardian*, 8 October 2011, p. 34.
36. 'Catholics send clear message to bring end to nuclear power,' *The Universe*, 4 December 2011, p. 4.
37. Ibid.

country's five nuclear reactors.[38] The Swiss government also decided not to build the three nuclear power stations which were in the pipeline. 20,000 people protested against nuclear power on 29 May 2011.[39] However, the Swiss authorities will have to move quickly to develop other sources of energy as nuclear power provided forty per cent of the country's electricity. Given the topography of the country, the Swiss will probably expand their use of hydroelectricity.

Since their last nuclear power plant is due to close in 2034, the Swiss government is being forced to find alternative sources of energy because they are heavily dependent on nuclear power. The government is focused on reducing energy use, especially in public buildings. Their target is a twenty-five per cent reduction by 2020. But there is also room for expansion in solar and wind energy, even though the latter is sometimes opposed by local communities which claim that wind turbines blight the landscape. One group of citizens in Canton Jura have taken legal action to block a wind-farm that could supply electricity to 40,000 people. Isabelle Chevalley, a Liberal Green parliamentarian, has little patience with such groups. 'We have to be prepared to make sacrifices,' like the people of Valais and Graubünden who 'sacrificed their valleys to build the big dams of which we are so proud today'.[40]

Italy
Following a referendum, Italy abandoned its nuclear programme in 1987, one year after the Chernobyl accident. As a result, the then government planned to wind-down Italy's existing nuclear reactors. The last one was shut in 1990. However, Prime Minister Silvio Berlusconi was still intent on reviving Italy's nuclear

38. Leigh Philips, 'Europe divided over nuclear power after Fukushima disaster,' *The Guardian*, 25 May 2011, http://www.guardian.co.uk/environment/2011/may/25/europe-divided-nuclear-power-fukushima/print.

39. Ian Sample, 'Japan crisis tests carbon emission cuts as nations end atomic option,' *The Guardian*, 30 May 2011, p. 6.

40. Luigi Jorio, swissinfo.ch, 'Switzerland is exploring sustainable energy sources(imagepoint.biz),' 5 January 2012, http://www.swissinfo.ch/eng/politics/internal_affairs/Walking_the_talk_on_renewable_energy.html.

programme.[41] He wanted to generate twenty-five per cent of Italy's electricity from French-designed nuclear reactors. But, in a referendum held on 12 and 13 June 2011, the Italian electorate once again voted against building any new nuclear power plants in high-risk seismic Italy.[42] The vote, which exceeded fifty per cent, means that the government will not now be able to restart its nuclear programme by 2014. Italy's biggest utility, Enel, had plans to start building nuclear power stations in the country, together with French power giant EDF in 2013. Those plans will now be mothballed. This vote against nuclear power is another nail in the nuclear power coffin.

United States

There was quite an amount of confusion at the headquarters of the Nuclear Regulatory Commission (NRC) in the hours and days following the Fukushima Daiichi accident. Some information came from the Japanese government, more trickled out from Tepco, but the bulk of the NRC's data came from new media (twitter, facebook etc.). On the second day of the crisis, one unnamed official at the NRC referred to 'unconfirmed reports of boiling' in the spent fuel pools.[43] Officials at the NRC were also aware and concerned about the safety of these nuclear reactors because they were similar to reactors in use in the US.

Nuclear power is important in the US as it provides about twenty per cent of the country's electricity. David Lochbaum, who is the director of the Nuclear Safety Project at the Union of Concerned Scientists (UCS) in the US, has raised questions about the nuclear safety record at many US reactors. Lochbaum trained as a nuclear engineer and worked in the industry for seventeen years. He left the industry when he failed to have the safety issues at the Sesquehanna nuclear power plant, Pennsylvania,

41. John Hooper, 'Blow to Berlusconi as nuclear power rejected,' *The Guardian*, 14 June 2011, p. 26.
42. Benedetta Brevini, *The Guardian*, 'The day Italians finally said no to Silvio Berlusconi,' 14 June 2011, http://www.guardian.co.uk/commentisfree/2011/jun/14/silvio-berlusconi-italian-referendum.
43. Matthew L. Wald, 'Records Show Confusion in US at Start of Japan's Atomic Crisis,' *The New York Times*, 20 February 2012.

investigated by either the company which operated the plant or the US Nuclear Regulatory Commission (NRC).

Lochbaum points out that most of the 104 nuclear reactors in the US are ageing rapidly. Despite this, the NRC has allowed nuclear reactors to increase the amount of electricity generated at the plants by twenty per cent, even though the reactors are not designed to handle such an increase. This is called 'power uprates' and is achieved by pumping an increased volume of cooling water through the plant, which, in turn, increases the wear and tear on pipes and other equipment, all of which are already almost forty years old.[44]

Another cause for worry is that the NRC has granted twenty licence extensions to thirty-nine nuclear reactors. Most of the remaining plants are also seeking such extensions. Despite these significant changes, Lochbaum claims that the NRC is cutting back on the amount and frequency of safety tests and inspections. Tests, which originally were carried out every four months are now carried out only once a year. Similarly, the annual inspections are now scheduled for the period when the reactor is shut down for refueling which happens about once every two years.[45] Lochbaum believes that, in the current climate of light-touch regulation and an ageing nuclear fleet, a serious accident in the US is almost inevitable.

The nuclear industry in the US has been seriously affected by what happened at Fukushima. After Fukushima, the plan to build a modern reactor project in Texas was cancelled. In the previous year, 2010, the proposal to build a nuclear power plant in Maryland was also dropped. It seems bizarre that the Bellefonte 1 nuclear reactor near Hollywood, Alabama, which was designed almost fifty years ago before the era of computers, might still be completed. The plant is owned by the Tennessee Valley Authority (TVA). At that time, the TVA stated that it would build two nuclear reactors on the Bellefonte site at a cost of $650 million. Building work only began in 1974. By 1988, the original budget

44. Karen Charman, 'Brave Nuclear World,' *World-Watch,* July / August 2006, p. 14.
45. Ibid.

estimate had been increased by a factor of six.[46] When demand for electricity dropped, the plant was mothballed. New possibilities opened up in 1994, when the TVA tried to sell electricity from the plant to the Philadelphia Electric Company. The deal was not pushed through. Three years later, the TVA tried to make a deal with the US Department of Energy which required a nuclear reactor to make tritium for the US nuclear weapons programme (Tritium is a radioactive isotope of hydrogen and is also known as hydrogen-3). The negotiations fell through when the tritium was sourced from another nuclear reactor owned by TVA.

In May 2011, TVA announced it would close eighteen antiquated, inefficient and polluting coal-burning plants in the next eighteen months. This is why the company is keen to complete Bellefonte 1. The Authority estimates that Bellefonte 1 could be up-and-running by 2020. The company is also bullish about the economics of the venture, even though, to date, it has cost $4 billion, and completing the plant could add another $4 to $5 billion to the final bill. Thomas Kilgore, who is the President of TVA and its chief executive, said that, in the long run, the company would make money from the plant. He claims that 'once you get the unit built, you've got inflation locked out.'[47] He believes that the demand for 'clean' energy will increase for two reasons. The US Environmental Protection Agency (EPA) is continuing to put pressure on dirty coal-fired plants to be shut down, and the price of natural gas is expected to increase, making nuclear energy more competitive.

Not everyone would agree with that analysis. Eric T. Beaumont, a nuclear expert and partner in Copia Capital, which is a Chicago-based investment firm, has said that completing Bellefonte 1 'doesn't seem like a prudent use of money'.[48] Environmentalists such as Louis A. Zeller, who is the science director for the Blue Ridge Environmental Defense League, has called the Bellefonte 1 the 'zombie reactor' because it is neither dead nor alive.[49] He is opposed to completing the reactor because it is too expensive and antiquated and it lies in an earthquake area.

---

46. Matthew L. Ward, 'Nuclear plant, left for dead, shows a pulse,' *The New York Times*, 15 June 2011. Accessed on 16 June 2011.
47. Ibid.
48. Ibid.
49. Ibid.

One important reason why TVA is interested in completing Bellefonte 1, despite its antiquated status, is that the plant has a construction licence which it obtained in 1974. Furthermore, the independent status of the authority means that there will be fewer obstacles to its completion. The TVA does not have to answer to state regulators and it has no shareholders, who might oppose the decision to complete the power plant. In 2010, the TVA allocated $248 million to explore the possibilities of completing the nuclear power station. It defies logic, but given the regulatory framework in the US, it is easier to get permission to complete a nuclear dinosaur like Bellefonte 1, than to get permission to build a newer more up-to-date nuclear power plant.

There is also significant political backing for completing the Bellefonte 1 plant. The Congressman from that area of Alabama is Representative Mo Brooks. He is backing the project and is on record as having said, 'more people have been killed by coal than nuclear, by far, when you talk about the mining, the pollution of the water and air pollution. Nuclear is not perfect, but it seems to be better than any alternative.'[50] The City Council in Scottsboro, a nearby town, and the Jackson County Commission have passed resolutions in favour of completing the reactor. One of the reasons why local people are supportive is that they believe that there will be jobs for about 2,800 people who will be needed to run the nuclear power plant.

The task force set up by the Nuclear Regulatory Commission in the US in the wake of the Fukushima Daiichi meltdowns, called for a 'redefining of the level of protection that is regarded as adequate'.[51] It calls for improvement in the US, based on what has been learnt from the nuclear accident in Japan. Those in the industry need to plan for separate accidents at adjacent reactors. Such planning has never happened before. It also called on the operators of nuclear installations to be sure that the 'hardened vents' which were added to reactors in recent times, to prevent hydrogen explosions, function properly. The report calls on operators to focus much more on the spent fuel pools and to make sure that there is a guaranteed supply of water to cool the rods.

50. Ibid.
51. http://www.nytimes.com/2011/07/13/science/earth/13nuke.html.

In June 2011, the governor of New York, Andrew M. Cuomo, warned the owners of the Indian Point nuclear power plant, Entergy that, for safety reasons, he wanted the two reactors in Westchester County to be shut down in 2013 and 2015, when their forty-year licences expire. Because Indian Point generates 16,000 gigawatt-hours per annum, which is one quarter of the electricity used in New York and Long Island, critics maintain that closing Indian Point without building any new electrical generation plant would lead to major power interruption between 2016 and 2020. Critics of the governor's plan also claim that shutting down the reactors would increase the wholesale price of electricity by about twelve per cent.[52] Many feel that the Nuclear Regulatory Agency has yet to fully understand the implications of what happened at Fukushima. In December 2011, the chairman of the US Nuclear Regulatory Commission, Gregory B. Jaczko told Bloomberg that, in the event of an accident, there would be enough time for people to be evacuated from the radioactive contaminated area. What he appears not to have understood is that 160,000 people who lived in Fukushima will not be able to return to their homes for twenty years or more. Hundreds of square miles around Chernobyl are still off-limits to people. If an accident happened at Indian Point, the people of New York City would have to be evacuated, with little possibility of returning to their homes in their lifetime. Many people criticise the Nuclear Regulatory Commission because it does not factor in such issues as permanent land contamination in 'its cost-benefits analyses for Indian Point and other nuclear plants in the United States.'[53]

France

There are fifty-eight nuclear reactors in France which generate almost seventy per cent of the country's electricity. The French built nuclear power plants in the 1960s and 1970s in order that the country might be less dependent on fossil fuel imports from the

52. Matthew L. Wald, 'If Indian Point Closes, Plenty of Challenges,' *The New York Times*, 13 July 2011.
53. Victor Gilinsky, 'Indian Point: The Next Fukushima?' *The New York Times*, 16 December 2011, http://www.nytimes.com/2011/12/17/opinion/is-indian-point-the-next-fukushima.html.

Middle East. After the accident at Fukushima, the French prime minister, Francois Fillon, asked the Nuclear Safety Authority to carry out a safety assessment at all of France's operating reactors.[54]

Though the majority of French people support nuclear power, there have been a number of accidents at nuclear power plants in France.[55] In July 2008, it emerged that a twenty-five-metre plastic pipe embedded in concrete was cracked at a nuclear plant in Romans-sur-Isère in the Drome region. This may have been leaking uranium for years. The Autorité de Sureté Nucleaire, the agency which oversees nuclear power plants, calculated that between 100 and 800 grams of uranium may have leaked from the broken pipe. The news broke just before the French government ordered safety tests in all of the country's nineteen nuclear power plants. This overall check was triggered by a leak which was discovered at an Areva nuclear installation in July 2008.[56] Martine Aubry, a member of the French Socialist Party, has stated that she is personally in favour of phasing out nuclear power, even though her party will have to decide on its nuclear power policy.[57] The French Green Party has called for a referendum on nuclear energy. The French national utility company which operates the nuclear reactors is fearful that it will not be able to meet the financial cost of upgrades which may be demanded as a result of the crisis at Fukushima.[58]

On 30 September 2011, a long article appeared in *The Guardian* entitled, 'The nuclear power plants that have survived Fukushima.'[59] The following is a summary of that article.

Anti-nuclear protestors in France are particularly concerned about the vulnerability of two reactors located at Fessenheim.

54. http://www.worldwatch.org/nuclear-power-after-fukushima, p. 41.
55. Fiona Harvey, 'Anxiety grows over use of nuclear energy,' *The Guardian*, 24 March 2011, p. 29.
56. Muriel Boselli, 'French nuclear plant may have been leaking "for years",' *The Irish Independent*, 19 July 2008, p. 26.
57. http://www.worldwatch.org/nuclear-power-after-fukushima p. 42.
58. Ibid.
59. The authors of the article are Hanan Alkiswany (Jordan), Lizette Damons (South Africa), Mike Ives (Vietnam), Theresa V. Ilano and Joel Adriano (Philippines), Ochieng' Ogodo (Kenya), Emeka Johnkingsley (Nigeria), Ma. Nehal Lasheen (Egypt), http://www.guardian.co.uk/environment/2011/sep/30/nuclear-power-fukushima.

These reactors are among the oldest in France and are located thirty feet beneath the dyke of a canal which runs close to the River Rhine. Water from the river is used as coolant in the nuclear power station. Critics claim that a break in the embankment could cause a catastrophic accident. Furthermore, the company which runs the power station has never studied what would happen if such an accident took place.[60] This oversight seems inexplicable, as the site is situated in an earthquake zone. Thirty miles to the south lies the city of Basel in Switzerland. In 1356, that city was totally destroyed by an earthquake. In January 2012, the French Nuclear Safety authority ordered EDF, the French national utility company, to study the potential consequences of a break in the dyke. It appears that the reactors were built to withstand an earthquake of 6.7 on the Richter scale. Swiss and German seismologists have calculated that the Basel earthquake registered 6.9 on the Richter scale. Their French counterparts claim that it was only 6.2 on the Richter scale.[61]

Those who are working to close the nuclear power plant also point out that the concrete containment vessels which surround the reactors at Fessenheim are a mere fraction of the thickness of those at the Fukushima Daiichi nuclear plant in Japan. The controversy surrounding the nuclear reactors became an issue in the French presidential election of May 2012. The Socialist candidate, and eventual victor, François Hollande, gave a pledge that he would shut the plant if elected president. President Nicolas Sarkozy pledged to continue to support France's extensive nuclear programme. Many of the 2,341 inhabitants of the nearby village also support keeping the plant open because of the financial benefits which the nuclear industry has brought to the village, in terms of jobs, good roads, shops, a public swimming pool and athletic centre.

The cost of nuclear power is among the main threats to nuclear power in France. In January 2012, ASN, the French nuclear authority warned that its nuclear supplier, EDF, will have to

---

60. Scott Sayare, 'Wishing Upon an Atom in a Tiny French Village,' *The New York Times*, 2 February 2012, http://www.nytimes.com/2012/02/03/world/europe/wishing-upon-an-atom-in-a-tiny-french-village.html.
61. Op. cit.

come up with around €10 billion to ensure that the vast web of fifty-eight nuclear power plants across France are made safe. Upgrading fifty-eight nuclear plants, many of which stretch back to the 1960s, in order that they comply with new international safety standards in the wake of the Fukushima disaster, will be costly.[62]

In a Greenpeace publication, *France's Nuclear Failures: The Great Illusion of Nuclear Power*, published in 2008, one chapter is devoted to problems arising from security concerns and secrecy. The author claims that in France a major problem with nuclear security is secrecy. It is claimed that, oftentimes, the authorities use secrecy as a pretext for creating a heightened level of security, while the problems in the industry are not being properly addressed. As the French Nuclear Safety Authority explained in 2001, counter-terrorist protection methods cannot by their very nature, be publicly communicated. Having become the first line of defence, in the eyes of the industry, secrecy must be protected at all costs. No internal analysis is disseminated and any external criticism is immediately denounced as playing into the hands of potential terrorists. More worrying, though, is the fact that it also blocks any discussion on nuclear or security issues.[63]

Jordan

Jordan plans to use nuclear power to deal with its energy shortages. Jordan's Atomic Energy Commission (JAEC) has set a target that sixty per cent of its energy needs would be provided by nuclear power by the year 2035. In 2011, Jordan spent one fifth of its gross domestic product buying energy from its Arab neighbours.

Energy is not the only problem facing Jordan. The country also has a growing problem with accessing fresh water. In this context, nuclear power would be used in desalination plants located in the Gulf of Aqaba in the southern part of the country. It also needs

---

62. 'France in bind over the soaring cost of nuclear safety,' http://blobcdn.ie-gallery.com/cdn/ie9slice/ie9.aspx?mainlang=en&maincountry=us.
63. 'France's Nuclear Failures: The Great Illusion of Nuclear Power,' Greenpeace International, Otto Heldringstraal 5, 1066 AZ Amsterdam. 2008, p. 13.

energy to pump this desalinated seawater to population centres in Amman, Irbid and Zarqa.

Like many other countries, Jordan re-evaluated its nuclear targets in the light of the Fukushima disaster, starting with the safety procedures for its nuclear reactor which was scheduled to begin construction in 2013. The country also considered more safety procedures for construction and for ongoing geological and environmental investigations.

According to Abdel-Halim Wreikat, Vice-Chairman of the JAEC, 'the government [will] not reverse its decision to build nuclear reactors in Jordan because of the Fukushima disaster. Our plant type is a third-generation pressurised water reactor, and it is safer than the Fukushima boiling water reactor.'[64] According to Wreikat, 'the nuclear option for Jordan at the moment is better than renewable energy options such as solar and wind, as they are still of high cost.' But some Jordanian researchers disagree. Ahmad Al-Salaymeth, director of the Energy Centre at the University of Jordan, says, 'the cost of electricity generated from solar plants comes down each year by about five per cent, while the cost of producing electricity from nuclear power is rising year after year.' He has called for more economic feasibility studies of the nuclear option.[65]

Ahmad Al-Malabeh, a professor in the Earth and Environmental Sciences Department of Hashemite University, points out that Jordan has other energy possibilities, besides going down the nuclear route. 'Jordan is rich, not only in solar and wind resources, but also in oil shale rock, from which we can extract oil that can cover Jordan's energy needs in the coming years, starting between 2016 and 2017 ... this could give us more time to have more economically feasible renewable energy.'[66]

South Africa

South Africa's Integrated Resource Plan (IRP) was unveiled in May 2010. It predicts that the consumption of electricity will increase

64. Op. cit, 'The Nuclear Power Plants that have survived Fukushima.'
65. Ibid.
66. Ibid.

from 260 terawatts per hour (TWh) to 454 TWh in 2030. Coal is the dominant source of energy for generating electricity in South Africa. In 2010, ninety per cent of South Africa's electricity was generated by coal-fired plants.[67] These coal-fired stations contribute significantly to South Africa's greenhouse gas emissions, which is why the South African government is keen on building nuclear power stations to generate electricity. According to the energy minister, Dipuo Peters, 'the first nuclear power unit will start generating in 2023, with the full 9.6 GW of new nuclear capacity on stream by 2030. This represents between six and nine new nuclear units (depending on the design chosen), located on three or four sites.' Elliot Mulane, communications manager for the South African Nuclear Energy Corporation, (NECSA) a public company established under the 1999 Nuclear Energy Act that promotes nuclear research, said the timing of the decision indicated 'the confidence that the government has in nuclear technologies'.[68]

Dipuo Peters, energy minister, also reiterated the commitment in her budget announcement earlier in May 2011. She stated that the South African government was 'still convinced that nuclear power is a necessary part of our strategy that seeks to reduce our greenhouse gas emissions through a diversified portfolio, comprising some fossil-based, renewable and energy efficiency technologies'.[69]

In what is obviously a related move, Rob Adam is moving from his strategic position as chief executive of the Nuclear Energy Corporation of South Africa (NECSA), to a private company, Aveng Group, which expects to benefit significantly from the one trillion rand nuclear expansion programme. The corporation he is leaving will be the gatekeeper for all technical co-operation agreements between the South African government and private corporations. Consequently, his move to the Aveng Group will give that company a distinct advantage over similar companies, which are involved in building or running nuclear power plants.

---

67. Dipuo Peters, 'Nuclear Power a key part of SA's future,' *Mail & Guardian*, 9–14 December 2011, p. 23.
68. Ibid.
69. Ibid.

Some of the other bidders for the nuclear contracts are critical of the fact that there is no cooling-off period between his work for the government and his taking up employment for a private firm with an interest in building nuclear power plants.

Adam's move has also been criticised by Civil Society Organisations (CSOs). David Fig, who as a critic of South Africa's nuclear industry has monitored the revolving door phenomenon of people like Rob Adam, who were at the centre of South Africa's nuclear development programme, moving to private nuclear companies where they can leverage enormous amounts of money for the private company. More worrying still is the fact that people (such as Adam) who 'understand the regulatory apparatus are able to take advantage of regulatory weaknesses to enhance their private interests once they cease working for the state sector.'[70] David Fig points out that Adam's move is not unique. For example, Roger Jardine was the former chairperson of the Nuclear Energy Corporation of South Africa and is now the chief executive of the Aveng Group. His company bid for the aborted nuclear tender in 2008 and will be bidding for nuclear contracts once again in 2012.[71]

James Larkin, director of the Radiation and Health Physics Unit at the University of the Witwatersrand, is of the opinion that South Africa will most likely opt for the relatively cheap, South Korean generation three-type reactors. He dismisses the role that renewable energy can play in meeting his country's energy needs, while also reducing greenhouse gas emissions. He argues that nuclear is capable of supplying eighty-five per cent of the base load (constantly needed) power supply, while solar energy can only produce between seventeen and twenty-five per cent.

He does acknowledge that financial concerns will probably put the brakes on building nuclear plants in the near future. 'The government has said yes but hasn't said how it will pay for it. This is going to end up delaying by fifteen years any plans to build a nuclear station.'[72]

---

70. Lionel Faull, 'Partnership too cosy for its own good,' *Mail & Guardian*, December 9–14, 2011, p. 12.

71. Ibid.

72. Ibid.

Vietnam

Moving to Asia, Vietnam hopes its first nuclear plant, Ninh Thuan, will be completed by 2020. It is to be built with support from the state-owned Russian energy company. In March 2012, scientists from the semi-governmental Japan Atomic Energy Agency, organised a training seminar on radiation for twenty young Vietnamese nuclear technicians. A twenty-seven-year-old student, Nguyen Xuan, told reporters that, 'Nuclear power is important for Vietnam's energy security but, like fire, it has two sides. We have to learn how to take advantage of its good side.'[73]

The Vietnamese government is actively promoting nuclear power as a solution to the country's energy needs. This means improving nuclear science and engineering programmes in its own universities and sending students to other countries to study all aspects of nuclear technology, including nuclear physics and nuclear regulatory programmes. This is a fast-track effort with the Vietnamese government planning to build one nuclear reactor by 2020 and a further nine by 2030.

Geologists such as Le Huy Minh, who is director of the Earthquake and Tsunami Warning Centre at Vietnam's Institute of Geophysics, have warned that the coastline of Vietnam can easily be affected by tsunamis in the South China Sea. Ninh Thuan is situated eighty to one hundred kilometres from a significant fault line. However, this does not seem to worry Vuong Huu Tan, president of the state-owned Vietnam Atomic Energy Commission. He told the state media in March that lessons from the Fukushima accident will help Vietnam to develop safe technologies.

John Morris, an Australia-based energy consultant, who has worked as a geologist in Vietnam, says the seismic risk for nuclear power plants in the country would not be 'a major issue' as long as the plants were built properly. Japan's nuclear plants are 'a lot more earthquake prone' than Vietnam's would be, he adds.[74] The difficulty is that Vietnam is still a very authoritarian state where civil society is not allowed to express its concerns or opposition to

73. Norimitsu Onishi, 'Vietnam's Nuclear Dreams Blossom Despite Doubts,' *The New York Times*, 1 March 2012, http://www.nytimes.com/2012/03/02/world/asia/vietnams-nuclear-dreams-blossom-despite-doubts.html.
74. Op. cit, 'The Nuclear Power Plants that have survived Fukushima.'

nuclear power. There is also widespread corruption which could lead to a weak regulatory regime. Such a regime was partly responsible for the catastrophe at the nuclear reactors at the Fukushima Daiichi power plant.

Hien Pham Duy, who is one of Vietnam's leading nuclear scientists, has dreamed for decades of bringing nuclear power to Vietnam. However, he is sceptical about the ambitious plans of the government because they are based on a 'lack of vigorous assessment of the inherent problems of nuclear power, especially those arising in less developed countries.'[75]

Tran Dai Phuc, a Vietnamese-French nuclear engineer who worked in the French nuclear industry for four decades and is now an advisor to Vietnam's Ministry of Science and Technology, the ministry in charge of nuclear power, has similar concerns. He is not worried about the reliability of the reactors' technology. His main concern is the lack of 'democracy as well as the responsibility of personnel, a culture of quality assurance and general safety regarding installation and impact on the environment'.[76]

Kenya

Like many other countries in the global south, Kenya needs energy to develop its economy. Less than half of the residents in the capital, Nairobi, have access to electricity and only two per cent in the rural areas have access to electricity. Kenya has the possibility of developing geothermal energy, but some argue that it should also go the nuclear route. In the same month as the Fukushima accident, inspectors from the International Atomic Energy Agency approved Kenya's application for its first nuclear power station (31 March 2011), a 35,000 megawatt facility to be built at a cost of Sh950 billion (US$9.8 billion) on a two-hundred-acre plot on the Athi Plains, about fifty kilometres from Nairobi. If work begins soon, the plant should be completed by 2022. The Kenyan government claims that this plant could satisfy all Kenya's energy needs until 2040.[77]

---

75. Ibid.
76. Ibid.
77. Ibid.

The Chairman of the Parliamentary Committee on Energy, Communication and Information, James Rege, takes a broader view than the official government line. He believes that geothermal energy from the Rift Valley project should be top of the country's energy strategy. Nuclear energy should be developed as a back-up to this form of energy.[78] Hydropower is limited by rivers running dry for part of each year and switching the country's arable land to biofuel production would threaten food supplies.

David Otwoma, secretary to the Energy Ministry's Nuclear Electricity Development Project, agrees that Kenya will not be able to industrialise without diversifying its energy mix to include more geothermal, nuclear and coal. Otwoma believes the expense of generating nuclear energy could one day be met through shared regional projects but, until then, Kenya has to move forward on its own. Rege insists that Kenya will take on board the lessons learned from the Fukushima accident.

Nigeria
Despite what happened at Fukushima, Nigeria is forging ahead with nuclear collaborations. Shamsideen Elegba, the chair of the Forum of Nuclear Regulatory Bodies in Africa, claims that Nigeria has the necessary regulatory system to operate nuclear facilities safely. This is an extraordinary claim for an oil-producing and exporting nation which cannot ensure an adequate supply of gasoline for its own citizens. I remember visiting Nigeria in 2009 and one was never sure whether a gasoline station had any supply of gasoline on a given day. People were forced to buy their gasoline on the black market. If Nigeria is so poor at supplying gasoline to its own citizens, the claim that they have the regulatory structure to deal with nuclear power seems far-fetched.

Elegba claims that 'Japan is one of the leaders not only in that industry, but in terms of regulatory oversight. They have a very rigorous system of licensing. We have to make a distinction between a natural event, or series of natural events and engineering infrastructure, regulatory infrastructure, and safety oversight.'[79]

---

78. Ibid.
79. Ibid.

In reality, it is now obvious that Japan had a very poor regulatory system. For Elegba to be claiming otherwise does not inspire confidence in Nigeria's ability to regulate a nuclear programme. Nigeria also has a notorious record for corruption and this is not a good foundation for an industry as potentially dangerous as the nuclear industry. In the Corruption Perception Index for 2011, produced by Transparency International, Nigeria ranked 143 out of a total number of 182 countries.

Nigeria is likely to recruit the Russian State Corporation for Atomic Energy, ROSATOM, to build its first proposed nuclear plant. A delegation from ROSATOM visited Nigeria (26 to 28 July 2011) and a bilateral document was finalised in 2011.

Nikolay Spassy, director general of the corporation, said during the visit: 'The peaceful use of nuclear power is the bedrock of development, and achieving [Nigeria's] goal of being one of the twenty most developed countries by the year 2020 would depend heavily on developing nuclear power plants.' ROSATOM points out that the International Atomic Energy Agency monitors and regulates power plant construction in previously non-nuclear countries.

But Nnimmo Bassey, executive director of the Environmental Rights Action/Friends of the Earth Nigeria (ERA/FoEN), said, 'We cannot see the logic behind the government's support for a technology that former promoters in Europe, and other technologically advanced nations, are now applying brakes to. What Nigeria needs now is investment in safe alternatives that will not harm the environment and the people. We cannot accept the nuclear option.'

Egypt
Egypt with its growing population, needs power to grow its economy. Unlike some of its Arab neighbours, it does not possess large reserves of fossil fuel. Egypt's nuclear programme goes right back to 1961 when it launched a research reactor. The country put on hold its nuclear programme after the nuclear accident at Chernobyl. By 2007, Egypt was keen to restart its nuclear programme. In the wake of the Spring Uprising in 2011,

and after the Fukushima accident, the Egyptian government postponed its tender for the construction of its first nuclear reactor. There are a lot of uncertainties in the current political situation in Egypt; with the election of Mohamed Morsi, of the Muslim Brotherhood, and the tensions between himself and the army and the country's Supreme Constitutional Court, proceeding with nuclear power plants will not be an immediate priority for the new president.

Yassin Ibrahim, chairman of the Nuclear Power Plants Authority and one of the authors of *The Guardian*'s article, said that: 'We put additional procedures in place to avoid any states of emergency but, because of the uprising, the tender will be postponed until we have political stability after the presidential and parliamentary elections at the end of 2011.'[80] Because of what happened at Fukushima, the 'design specifications for the Egyptian nuclear plant (will) take into account resistance to earthquakes and tsunamis, including those greater in magnitude than any that have happened in the region for the last four thousand years. The reactor type is of the third generation of pressurised water reactors, which have not resulted in any adverse effects to the environment since they began operation in the early sixties'.[81]

According to Ibrahim El-Osery, a consultant in nuclear affairs and energy at the country's Nuclear Power Plants Authority, Egypt's limited resources of oil and natural gas will run out in twenty years, and renewable energy supplied only two per cent of the country's needs in 2010. It is estimated that Egypt has 15,000 tonnes of untapped uranium.

Egypt's ambition to go nuclear is not merely about securing a supply of energy. It also has political connotations according to Nadia Sharara, professor of mineralogy at Assiut University. 'Owning nuclear plants is a political decision in the first place, especially in our region and any state that has acquired nuclear technology has political weight in the international community.'[82]

---

80. Ibid.
81. Ibid.
82. Ibid.

India

In November 2011, thousands of fishermen, along with a number of Catholic nuns and priests, in two Tamil Nadu dioceses protested against the building of a nuclear plant in the southern Indian state. One of the reactors is set to begin production in 2012.[83] The Koodankulam Nuclear plant which has just been completed is situated in the Tirunelveli district of the southern state of Tamil Nadu. The plans to build this nuclear power station with two reactors goes back to a treaty signed by the then Prime Minister, Rajiv Gandhi, and the Soviet President Mikhail Gorbachev on 20 November 1988. The construction work was stalled for over a decade due to the political and economic upheaval in Russia after the fall of Communism and the break up of the Soviet Union in 1991. The United States also objected to the building of the power plant on the grounds that the agreement did not meet the terms of the 1992 Nuclear Supplies Group.

The plant was to begin production in December 2011. However, as of February 2012, it was still idle. This has led to an intervention by the Russian Ambassador to India, Alexander M. Kadakin, who said that 'The machines have to start working now. Because after several weeks you will have to spend much more time and money to maintain them. You will pay for nothing. They will be idle but you have to pay for their maintenance.'[84]

Church leaders from the diocese of Tuticorin and Kottar are calling the nuclear plant 'a disaster waiting to happen', in the light of what happened in Fukushima in March 2011. Bishop Yuvon Ambroise of Tuticorin and chairperson of the Catholic Office for Justice, Peace and Development (JPD) said, that 'Russian nuclear technology has failed in Chernobyl, why should we use it here to endanger our lives?'[85] The bishop also said that India should follow the example of both Germany and Japan where nuclear technology is being phased out. Bishop Peter Remigius of Kottar supported

83. 'Protesters take aim at nuclear plant,' UCAN News, 20 September 2011, http://www.ucanews.com/2011/09/20/protesters-take-aim-at-nuclear-plant.
84. 'Koodankulam Nuclear Power Plant should start working now, says Russia,' *The Economic Times*, 15 February 2012, http://articles.economictimes.india-times.com/2012-0215/news/31063357_1_protests-power-station-kalpakkam.
85. Ibid.

his fellow bishop and said that 'our lives are in danger because of the nuclear plant'.

Many of the protesters pointed out that the nuclear power plant was built in an area which was affected by the Asian tsunami that struck the region in December 2004. The noted social activist, Medha Patkar, said questions remained over why the government had approved the facility in an inhabited area despite environmental concerns.[86] State officials have said, however, that Prime Minister Manmohan Singh has assured the protesters that a federal minister would be appointed to meet with protesters and 'assuage their fears about the nuclear plant'.

In India, there are plans to build a prototype of a nuclear power plant using thorium as the fuel source. The claim is that this will make the nuclear plant safer. This is not the first time scientists have focused on using thorium for nuclear power plants. Thorium is much more abundant on earth than uranium and will not result in large quantities of carbon dioxide being released into the environment. Thorium is a radioactive element which, theoretically, could produce large amounts of electricity. According to Ratan Kumar Sinha, director of the Bhabha Atomic Research Centre (BARC) in Mumbai, he and his team were drawing up plans for the new large scale experimental thorium reactor. He went on to say that 'the basic physics and engineering of the thorium-fuelled advanced heavy water reactor (AHWR) are in place, and the design is ready.'[87]

During late 2011 and early 2012, Ratan Kumar Sinha and his team were examining suitable spots for such a reactor. It will probably be built close to an existing nuclear power plant. It is expected that the plant will take six years to complete, so it should be ready by the end of this decade. The reactor is designed to produce 300MW of electricity. This is about half the output from a conventional uranium-based nuclear reactor.

One advantage of using thorium is that the waste from thorium plants is radioactive for hundreds of years instead of thousands of

---

86. Ibid.
87. Maseeh Raham, 'The nuclear option: India pins hopes on cleaner, thorium-powered plants', *The Guardian*, 2 November 2011, p. 23.

years, as is the situation with using uranium. Another plus for thorium reactors over uranium is that uranium is very scarce and is being quickly depleted, whereas thorium is abundant, especially in India. It is also the case that thorium will not lead to a runaway chain reaction that can precipitate a nuclear disaster. It is not the first time that scientists have looked at using thorium instead of uranium. Quite a significant amount of research was carried out on thorium reactors in the United States in the 1950s and 1960s, but, as yet, no thorium-based power plant has ever been built.

CHAPTER FOUR

Light-Touch Regulation

Governments, Regulators and Corporations often Cover-Up Nuclear Accidents

The Japanese nuclear crisis lifted the lid off this very secretive industry. Many people in Japan and elsewhere were aware that building nuclear power stations in an area prone to large earthquakes and tsunamis was irresponsible. In 2006, Professor Katsuhiko Ishibashi, an expert in urban safety in Japan, resigned from the nuclear power advisory body, because he believed that building a nuclear power plant, such as Fukushima, in an earthquake zone could lead to disaster. In 2007, he said that the government, powerful corporations and the academic community had seriously underestimated the dangers posed by earthquakes. He claimed that nuclear power plants at Onagawa, Shika and Kashiwazaki-Kariwa were all hit by earthquakes stronger than they were designed to withstand.[1] An earthquake measuring 6.8 on the Richter scale caused a fire at the Kashiwazaki reactor on 16 July 2007. The fire burned for two hours and radioactive water leaked from the power station. No action was taken in the wake of this incident, even though Professor Katsuhiki had warned that many of the nuclear reactors in Japan had 'fatal flaws' in their design.[2]

In response to the lax oversight by the Japanese Nuclear Regulator, Mr Kaieda, the trade and industry minister, said that the Japanese government could give the nuclear regulatory agency more independence by early 2012. Yukiya Amano, the secretary general of the International Atomic Energy Agency (IAEA), said that the nuclear regulators must be 'genuinely independent'.[3] There was widespread criticism of the way the Japanese government handled the accident at Fukushima in the immediate aftermath of the earthquake and tsunami. Too much latitude was given to the

---

1. Robin McKie, 'Tokyo ministers ignored expert's warning on risk of building reactors that had "fatal flaws",' *The Observer*, 13 March 2011, p. 3.
2. Ibid.
3. Martin Fackler, 'Japan Plans Nuclear Regulatory Reform,' *The New York Times*, 21 June 2011.

operator, Tepco, and the nuclear regulatory agency seemed to be shielding the company rather than dealing with the accident. One of the factors which led to the disaster at Fukushima was the cosy relationship between the Japanese government, nuclear regulators and nuclear power corporations. Just one month before the earthquake hit the north-east of Japan, the Japanese government regulator approved a ten year extension to the six reactors at Fukushima, despite warning about the safety of the plants. The regulator pointed out that there were stress cracks in the backup diesel-powered generator at reactor number 1. These findings were published on the website of the Japanese nuclear regulatory agency. Nevertheless, the regulator approved the extension, which raises very serious questions about the unhealthy relationship between the power plant operators and the Japanese nuclear regulators. Regulators said that 'maintenance management was inadequate' and the 'quality of inspection was insufficient'.[4]

Louli Andreev, a Russian nuclear expert, who organised the clean-up of Chernobyl in 1986, was critical of Tepco's behaviour. The corporation cut costs by placing spent fuel rods too close to each other in the pools near the reactor. He stated that 'the Japanese were very greedy and they used every square inch of the space. But when you have a dense placing of spent fuel in the basin, you have a high possibility of fire if the water is removed from the basin.'[5] Pressure on Tepco management to cut costs meant that the Fukushima plant contained 4,000 uranium assemblies. This is three times the amount of radioactive material normally kept at a nuclear plant. The assemblies were kept in pools of circulating water. The drop in water levels when the pumps were overwhelmed by the tsunami caused the rods to overheat and led to the release of radioactive particles into the atmosphere.[6]

4. Hiroko Tabuchi, Norimitsu Onishi and Ken Belson, 'Japan Extended Reactor's Life, Despite Warning,' *The New York Times*, 21 March 2011, www.nytimes.com /2011/)3/22/world/asia/22nuclear.html.
5. Julian Borger, 'Russian expert accuses watchdog of negligence,' *The Guardian*, 16 March 2011, p. 6.
6. Justin McCurry, 'Safety lapses at stricken nuclear plant revealed,' *The Guardian*, 23 March 2011, p. 3.

In Japan, the pressure to extend the life of ageing nuclear power plants came from a desire to reduce the country's reliance on fossil fuel. One third of Japan's electricity is generated by nuclear power stations and it was hoped to increase that to fifty per cent by 2020. Eisaku Kato, the former governor of Niigata Prefecture, where Fukushima is situated, was critical of the nuclear regulators. He believes that 'an organisation (the regulatory agency) which is inherently untrustworthy is charged with ensuring the safety of Japan's nuclear plants'.[7] In 2002, the president of Japan's largest power company was forced to resign when he and other officials were suspected of falsifying the safety records at nuclear power plants.[8]

The accident at Fukushima was not the first nuclear accident in Japan. In fact, the industry has been plagued by accidents, plant closures, major cost overruns and radiological releases. In December 1995, when sodium coolant leaked from the Fast Breeder Reactor in Monju, Japan, the nuclear industry attempted to cover up the full extent of the damage.

Attempts to Cover-Up
Many commentators believe that the Japanese authorities at first tried to cover up the severity of what happened at Fukushima. Initially, the government was claiming that, while the explosion had destroyed the exterior wall of the building, there was no damage to the actual metal which housed the reactor. Even on 16 March 2011, the Japanese government's spokesman, Yukio Edano, continued to insist that contamination was low, even within the twenty kilometre exclusion zone.[9] Jeffery Kluger of *Time Magazine* accused Edano of 'speaking gobbledygook'.[10]

Cover-Ups in the US
The Japanese government is not the only government to be involved in cover-ups when it comes to dealing with nuclear

7. Ibid., p. 3.
8. Robin McKie, op. cit., p. 3.
9. David McNeill, 'Emperor breaks his silence as nuclear panic engulfs Japan,' *The Independent*, 17 March 2011, p. 4.
10. Jeffrey Kluger, 'Fear Goes Nuclear,' *Time* (magazine), 28 March 2011, p. 27.

power. It took the US government thirty-seven years to reveal that radioactive iodine had been discharged at the Hanford Nuclear Reservation in Washington State. In 1979, the largest radioactive spill in US history took place at the United Nuclear Mill at Church Rock, New Mexico. One hundred million gallons of radioactive material contaminated the drinking water for over 1,700 Navajo people and their livestock. In the aftermath of the accident, the company refused to supply emergency food and water for the people who were affected by the spillage. Rather than seeking to clear up the mess and minimise the damage, the company stonewalled for nearly five years before agreeing to pay a paltry $525,000 out of court settlement to the victims.[11]

On 30 March 1979, in the immediate aftermath of the accident at Three Mile Island in Pennsylvania in the US, the authorities attempted to allay public anxiety by declaring that the amount of radioactivity released into the environment was 'not dangerous.'[12]

Dangerous Earthquakes and Fault Lines
The nuclear safety debate in the US will be focused on the two nuclear power plants which are situated in California. Both of these nuclear plants are situated near geological fault lines. Diablo Canyon is situated twelve miles south-west of San Luis Obispo which is near the Hosgri fault. This fault was only discovered in 2008. San Onofre, in San Diego County, is close to the Oceanside and Newport–Inglewood/Rose Canyon fault. Both of these plants were built to withstand an earthquake measuring 7 to 7.5 on the Richter scale. However, Robert Alvarez of the Institute for Policy Studies, has pointed out that the 1906 earthquake which destroyed much of San Francisco measured 8.3 on the Richter scale. This is significantly beyond what the engineers who de- signed the facilities had predicted.[13] It is worth remembering that thirty of the nuclear reactors currently operating in the US are similar in design to the one at Fukushima.

---

11. Michael Brooks, 'Is it all over for nuclear?' *NewScientist*, 22 April 2006, p. 37.
12. Harold Jackson, 'US nuclear plant leak worst ever,' *The Guardian*, 31 March 2011, p. 32.
13. Sharon Begley and Andrew Murr, 'Disaster Plan,' *The Irish Examiner*, 22 March 2011, p. 13.

Bill Ellsworth, who is the Chief Scientist for the Earthquake and Hazard Program at the US Geological Survey, adds that 'we know that earthquakes as large or larger than [Japan's] have occurred in the past in the US and will almost certainly occur in the future.'[14] There are very serious doubts that the authorities in California are prepared for such an eventuality. Richard Allen, the associate director of the Seismological Laboratory at the University of California, Berkeley, said that it would take about $80 million to put in place a first class earthquake and tsunami warning system in the next five years. However, with the serious cut backs in the federal budget, there is little possibility of that amount of money becoming available any time soon.

A new map listing the various geologic faults east of Denver was published at the end of January 2012. It was a joint project of the US Department of Energy and the Electric Power Research Institute, which is a non-profit-making utility. The work had begun before the quake at the Fukushima Daiichi plant in March 2011, but the accident lent an urgency to the project. A further cause for concern was the earthquake near Mineral, Virginia, in the summer of 2011, which shook the twin-reactor plant beyond the extent which its designers had anticipated. While the new maps are valuable, they do not calculate the risk of damage to nuclear reactors. That is still left to the owners of the utility. According to a spokesperson for the US Nuclear Regulatory Commission, Scott Brunel, 'the model is a first step'.[15]

One worrying feature, from a geological perspective, is that earthquakes can occur in places far removed from where the Earth's tectonic plates meet. Between 16 December 1811 and 7 February 1812, a series of massive earthquakes hit the entire Mississipi Valley from the Gulf of Mexico to the city of Cairo, which is located in Southern Illinois at the confluence of the Mississippi and Ohio Rivers. The seismic activity was centred on the city of New Madrid in Missouri. The 1811–1812, quakes

---

14. Ibid.
15. Matthew L. Wald, 'Map of Earthquake Risks is Updated,' *The New York Times*, 31 January 2012, http://www.nytimes.com/2012/02/01/science/earth/map-of-earthquake-risks-is-updated.html.

registered between 7 and 8 on the Richter scale and affected about 129,000 square kilometres or 50,000 square miles of the US.[16] The New Madrid fault line straddles a number of states, including Illinois, Indiana, Missouri, Arkansas, Kentucky, Tennessee and Mississippi. Even though those earthquakes wreaked enormous damage, with waves on the river overwhelming boats and tossing other boats high up on the banks of the river, the human damage was minimal, as very few people lived there at the time. Today, more than fifteen million people live in the quake zone. A similar seismic event today would displace about 7.2 million people. The authors of the survey believe that there 'is a twenty-five to twenty per cent chance of a magnitude 6 or larger quake hitting the New Madrid area in the next fifty years'.[17] There are fifteen nuclear plants in the area of the New Madrid fault line. In 2009, the ten kilometre long Marianna fault was discovered in Arkansas. Haydar-Al-Shukri, of the University of Arkansas, claims that a magnitude 7 earthquake could take place in that area.

The massive earthquake in Shaanxi province in China in 1556, also took place far from the boundaries of tectonic plates. Scientists are now beginning to realise that these 'intraplate' earthquakes are not as infrequent as previously thought. Mian Liu, who works at the University of Missouri in Columbia, has been studying intraplate earthquakes which have occurred in China over the past 2,000 years. He believes that these earthquakes 'hop around haphazardly. Areas of violent shock become quiescent; previously docile areas suddenly become active.'[18]

Flooding

Earthquakes are not the only problems threatening nuclear installations. In June 2011, the floods on the Missouri River threatened two nuclear power plants on the river. At Cooper Station, workers spent days protecting the plant from the rising flood waters. Eighty miles away, the Fort Calhoun nuclear plant came under similar pressure on 26 June 2011. During the attempt

16. Ferris Jabr, 'Quake Escape,' *NewScientist*, 14 February 2012, pp. 34–35.
17. Ibid.
18. Ibid., p. 36.

to protect the plant, a worker punctured a 2,000-foot rubber berm which had been put in place to protect the nuclear power plant. The flood waters threatened electrical equipment, so this necessitated cutting the power supply to the larger grid and using the stand-by diesel engines to keep power flowing to the reactor. Two days later, the water level stabilised at 1,006.5 feet, according to the Omaha Public Power District, the operator of the Fort Calhoun plant.[19] Every doorway was barricaded with four-foot-high water-barriers that are intended to survive the pressure, even if an earthquake hits during a flood. Officials at the nuclear plant admitted that flooding is always a potential risk for nuclear reactors, but the threat has a higher profile lately because of the tsunami which hit the Fukushima Daiichi reactors. TV footage of floods at the front and back door of a nuclear power plant has done little to increase the confidence of the public that nuclear power is safe.

In Britain, it is estimated that twelve of its nineteen nuclear sites are at risk of flooding. The UK Department for Environment, Food and Rural Affairs (DEFRA) has assessed that nine sites are now at risk while others are in danger from rising sea levels and storms in the future. Officials from DEFRA found that all the sites for eight of the proposed nuclear power plants are in the danger zone. At present, Hinkley Point has a low risk of flooding but due to climate change it will face a high risk, both from flooding and erosion in the future. According to David Crichton, a flood specialist at the Hazard Research Centre at University College London, flooding at some of the existing nuclear power stations 'will make decommissioning expensive and difficult'.[20]

Access to water to cool nuclear power plants is also a problem because nuclear power plants use enormous quantities of water. On 20 January 2012, a state engineer with the Utah Division of Water Rights approved two applications that allow Blue Castel Holdings to extract 53,600 acre-feet of water from the Green River each year as coolant for the proposed nuclear power plant. That

19. Matthew L. Wald, 'Concern at Nebraska Reactors as Floodwaters Rise,' *The New York Times*, 26 June 2011.
20. Rob Edwards, 'Nuclear Power sites face flood and erosion risks,' *The Guardian*, 8 March 2012, p. 6.

amounts to seventeen billion gallons of water per year, enough to meet the needs of a city with a population of 100,000.[21] Even today, Utah is a very dry state and the predictions are that climate change is going to make it even drier. On the east coast of the US, few people are aware that the Indian Point nuclear power plant, which supplies electricity for New York City, uses about 2.5 billion gallons of water from the Hudson River daily. The impact of nuclear power on fresh water sources is seldom factored into the equation when assessing the benefits and risks associated with nuclear power.[22]

Fires

Fires also pose threats to nuclear installations. In June 2011, fires burned to within a few miles of a dump site near Los Alamos, where scientists connected with the Manhattan Project had developed the atomic bomb during the Second World War. The dump contained 20,000 barrels of plutonium-contaminated waste, which included contaminated clothes and equipment. The director of operations at the laboratory assured the public that there was no immediate threat to public safety 'even in extreme conditions'.[23]

Lax Regulations

Many people claim that there is a very lax nuclear regulatory regime in the US. Andrew C Revkin, from *The New York Times*, wrote that, 'nuclear power is a textbook example of the problem of "regulatory capture", in which an industry gains control of an agency meant to regulate it. "Regulatory capture" can be countered only by vigorous public scrutiny and Congressional oversight, but, in the thirty-two years since Three Mile Island, interest in nuclear regulation has declined precipitously.'[24]

21. Dawn Stover, 'In hot water: The "other" global warming,' *Bulletin of the Atomic Scientists*, 15 February 2012. http://www.thebulletin.org/node/9013.
22. Ibid.
23. 'Fire service scrambles to protect US nuclear weapons lab from blaze,' *The Irish Times*, 30 June 2011, p. 11.
24. Ibid.

Even after the Fukushima crisis, many people claim that a similar accident could not happen in the US, partly because there is not that much seismic activity there. The Federal Agency for ensuring that nuclear power plants in the US are operated safely is the Nuclear Regulatory Commission (NRC). The Union of Concerned Scientists reviewed that Commission's work in a report published in March 2011, before the crisis in Japan. The report entitled, *The NRC and Nuclear Power Safety in 2010* was written by a nuclear engineer called David Lochbaum. He examined fourteen 'near misses' at US nuclear power stations during 2010 and he evaluated the NRC response in each case. He found that there were 'a variety of shortcomings, such as inadequate training, faulty maintenance, poor design and failure to investigate problems thoroughly'.[25] The report gives examples of effective and ineffective responses from the nuclear industry.

A task force created in the US in April 2011, after the nuclear accident in Fukushima, claimed that nuclear safety rules in the US did not adequately weigh the risk that a single event could knock out both the normal energy supply from the electricity grid and the back-up emergency generators, as happened in Fukushima.[26] Officials from the NRC claimed that the safety equipment which was installed at US nuclear plants, especially since the 11 September 2001 attack in New York and Washington, was not properly maintained or inspected as diligently as it should have been. Charlie Miller, chairperson of the task force, pointed out that the vents which had been added to US nuclear reactors to protect against a hydrogen explosion might not work, as happened at Fukushima when it proved impossible to open the vents.

There seems to be major division within the NRC. In December 2011, four members of the NRC told a committee of the House of Representatives in Washington that their chairman, Gregory B. Jaczko, 'withheld information from them, berated the agency's professional staff, reduced female employees to tears

25. http://ucsusa.org/nuclear power/nuclear power risk-safety/nrc-and-nuclear-power-2010.html. Downloaded on 19 April 2011.
26. Matthew L. Wald, 'Nuclear Plants Safety Rules Inadequate, Group Says,' *The New York Times*, 15 June 2011, www.nytimes.com/2011106116/business/energy-environment116nrc.html.

with abusive comments and created a "chilled" atmosphere that was hurting the agency's ability to function'.[27] It was also disclosed that the decision not to proceed with a nuclear waste disposal project at Yucca Mountain in the Nevada desert was taken for political reasons, not technical ones. Senator Harry Reid from Nevada, leads the Democratic majority in the US Senate and he vigorously opposed building the nuclear dump in his state. Dr Jaczko formerly worked for Senator Reid.[28]

New Nuclear Reactor Approved for the United States
No new reactor has been built in the United States since the Three Mile Island accident in 1979. In December 2011, Westinghouse Electric Company unveiled a new reactor AP1000, and received approval from the Nuclear Regulatory Commission (NRC). Four of these reactors are currently being built in China. Utilities in the states of Georgia and South Carolina have applied for permission to build these newly-designed reactors in their respective states. According to Gregory B. Jaczko, 'the design provides enhanced safety margins through the use of simplified, inherent passive, or other innovative safety and security functions, and also has been assessed to ensure it could withstand damage from an aircraft impact without significant release of radioactive material.'[29] The Union of Concerned Scientists (UCS), however, voiced concerns about the design because of the lack of real-world testing of the reactor. Furthermore, the UCS point out that the AP1000 has 'less robust containment systems, less redundancy in safety systems, and fewer safety-grade structures, systems and components'.[30]

On 9 February 2012, The Nuclear Regulatory Commission (NRC) granted a licence to the Southern Company to build and

27. Matthew L. Wald, 'Leader of Nuclear Agency Litany of Objections,' *The New York Times,* 14 December 2011, http://www.nytimes.com/2011112/15/us/nrc-leader-gregory-jaczko-hears-litany-of-complaints.html.
28. Ibid.
29. Vegan Verve, 'Nuclear Regulatory Commission Approves New Reactor Design For Use In US,' 23 December 2011, http://www.aboutmyplanet.com-science-technology/nuclear-regulatorycommission-approves-new-reactor-design-for-use-in-u-sl.
30. Ibid.

operate two reactors at Alvin W. Wogtle Nuclear Power Station near Augusta in Georgia.[31] It is now more than thirty years since the last reactor was built in the United States. The project is estimated to cost $14 billion dollars. Even as the company was applying for the licence, $4 billion had already been spent on preparing the site and digging out the foundations. While four members of the NRC voted in favour of granting the licence, Gregory B. Jaczko opposed the application and voted against the project because some of the safety improvements which were sought by the NRC in response to the Fukushima Daiichi disaster may not be incorporated in the design. 'I cannot support issuing this licence as if Fukushima had never happened,' said Mr Jaczko.[32]

A coalition of anti-nuclear groups said they would file suit to block the commission's decision because the lessons of Fukushima had not been applied to the design. Business groups, including the United States Chamber of Commerce and the American Public Power Association, offered fervent praise.

Most other utility companies in the US believe that the Southern Company is betting that electricity prices will rise significantly over the next few years, thus making the generation of electricity from nuclear reactors profitable. Others are not convinced by this argument. They point to the huge cost over-runs which dogged the nuclear industry in the 1960s, 1970s and 1980s and to the low cost of natural gas in 2012.

International Atomic Energy Agency
The regulatory record of the International Atomic Energy Agency (IAEA) needs to be assessed in the light of its response to both the Fukushima and Chernobyl disasters. The Secretary General of the Agency is Yukyia Amano. He is Japanese and it is alleged that he secured the top job after vigorous lobbying by the Japanese

---

31. Matthew L. Wald, 'Federal Regulators Approve Two Nuclear Reactors in Georgia,' *The New York Times*, 10 February 2012, http://www.nytimes.com/20 12/02110/business/energy-environment/2-newreactors-approved-in-georgia.html.
32. Ibid.

government. According to *The Guardian* correspondent, Julian Borger, it took a long time for the agency to issue credible statements about what was happening at the Fukushima Daiichi power plant.[33] In response to sustained criticism from the media, IAEA took a leaf out of Adam's book and blamed someone else! In what was seen as a rebuke to the Japanese Prime Minister, Naota Kan, Yukiya Amano said, 'We do not have all the details of the information so what we can do is limited. I am trying to further improve the communication.'[34]

In the next chapter, Dr Helen Caldicott, a medical doctor who is opposed to nuclear power, criticises the IAEA's record in relation to the Chernobyl nuclear disaster. It is important to remember that the IAEA's function is first and foremost to 'accelerate and enlarge the contribution of atomic energy to peace, health and prosperity throughout the world'.[35] Having the IAEA regulating the nuclear industry is like having foxes supervising the welfare of chickens!

---

33. Julian Bolger, 'Russian expert accuses watchdog of negligence,' *The Guardian*, 16 March 2011, p. 6.

34. Andrew Buncombe, 'No Home. No Help. No Hope,' *The Independent*, 17 March 2011, p. 2.

35. Helen Caldicott, 'How nuclear apologists mislead the world over radiation,' *The Guardian*, 11 April 2011, http://www.guardian.co.uk/environment/2011104111/nuclear-apologists-radiation.

CHAPTER FIVE

Nuclear Power:
A History of Cover-ups, Deception and Incompetence

Britain

On 8 October 1957, a fire in the graphite reactor's core at Windscale, now named Sellafield, burned a substantial amount of uranium. The fire raged for almost three days and sent a plume of caesium, iodine and polonium–201 across Britain and Northern Europe.[1] Milk affected by radiation was dumped for months after the accident. However, farm workers who were picking potatoes in the area were not warned of the risks from the fallout.[2] According to a report produced by Sir William Penney, a scientist who had worked on the Manhattan Project,[3] the fault which caused the fire happened because of deficiencies in the technology used in the design of the cartridges. Since such an admission would have undermined the faith of the US in Britain's ability to handle nuclear power, the then prime minister, Harold Macmillan, ordered a complete cover-up and Penney's report was withdrawn. Later, Macmillan issued a distorted version of Penney's report in a White Paper. To muddy the waters further, Penney asserted on a radio programme that the accident was caused primarily by the operators at the time. This made the fire seem like a minor accident, caused primarily by incompetent technicians. Naturally, this incensed the technicians who worked at the plant and who had done everything in their power to contain the fire, at great risk to their own health. A postscript was added when the Americans investigated what had happened and the managers at Windscale took full credit for the actions which were taken to control the fire. Tim Touhy was deputy manager at Windscale when the fire occurred. It is now agreed that his

---

1. Michael McCarthy, 'After decades of lies, nuclear reassurances now fall on deaf ears,' *The Independent*, 16 March 2011, p. 2.
2. Paul Brown, 'Windscale's terrible legacy,' *The Guardian*, 26 August 1990, p. 9.
3. The Manhattan Project was a research and development programme that produced the first atomic bomb during the Second World War.

leadership was crucial in ensuring that the accident was not more catastrophic. While he was allowed to be present at the investigation, he was not allowed to speak. Afterwards, when asked for his comments he said, 'What a shower of bastards.'[4]

In October 2007, John Garland, formerly a researcher at the UK Atomic Energy Authority, admitted that, 'we have to double our estimates of amounts that were released.'[5] Twice in the past fifty years, scientists have increased their estimation of the number of people who probably contracted cancer because of the radioactive material released from Windscale. In 2007, Professor Richard Wakeford, an epidemiologist at Manchester University, said that it was impossible to determine which individual cancer was linked to the Windscale accident.[6] More than fifty years on from the accident, the damaged reactor at Sellafield still presents a formidable challenge. The UK Atomic Energy Authority (AEA) has designed robots, which are capable of dismantling the radioactive core. Richard Roper, the AEA programme manager in 2007, stated that the aim was to decommission the plant by the year 2060.[7] According to Barry Hickey, the site manager at Sellafield, the cost of dismantling Windscale will be borne by the taxpayer. Much of the money will come from the budget of the Ministry of Defence which 'benefited' from the production of plutonium for nuclear weapons.[8]

Many buildings within the sprawling complex of Sellafield are very dangerous. George Beveridge, the deputy managing director of Sellafield, told The Observer's science editor, Robin McKie, that B30, a large building in the centre of the Sellafield complex, is 'the most hazardous industrial building in western Europe. The reason is simple: it contains piles of old nuclear reactor parts and decaying fuel rods. The really worrying aspect is that the experts in

---

4. http://www.envocare.co.uk/windscale_disaster.html. Downloaded on 25 March 2011.
5. Robin McKie, 'Windscale radiation twice as bad as predicted,' The Observer, 27 October 2007, p. 25.
6. Ibid.
7. Rob Edwards, 'Windscale fallout blew right across Europe,' NewScientist, 6 October 2007, p. 11.
8. Paul Brown, op. cit., p. 9.

Sellafield do not know either the age or the exact nature of what is being stored'.[9] But B30 is not the only dangerous building on the Sellafield site. Next door, according to Beveridge, is the second most hazardous industrial building in Europe. Both buildings are now crumbling. Engineers reckon that the cleanup for these two sites alone could reach £50 billion. Dr Paul Howarth, executive director of Dalton Nuclear Institute at Manchester, claims that the British taxpayer at present pays £1.5 billion a year cleaning up Sellafield's waste problem and that they will have to continue to pay this amount for years to come.

Part of the reason that the Sellafield site is so dangerous is that the reactors known as Pile 1 and Pile 2 were not originally built to generate electricity but to produce plutonium for the British Army, which wanted to have its own independent nuclear deterrent as the Cold War intensified in the early 1950s. In order to achieve this goal of having atomic weapons, Sellafield was built at breakneck speed. McKie outlines the appalling consequences: 'those scientists had no time to think about the waste produced by their atomic bomb programme, a point starkly demonstrated by another Sellafield legacy building, B41. It still stores the aluminium cladding for the uranium fuel rods that were burned inside Pile 1.' That uranium posed serious disposal problems when it was removed, in a highly radioactive state, from the two reactors, as their fuel was decommissioned and their plutonium extracted. So scientists hit on what seemed to be an ingenious solution: they would dump it in a silo.[10] They dropped the nuclear waste into the silo and allowed it to sink to the bottom. Soon they realised that pieces of aluminum and magnesium could catch fire and cause widespread contamination. To prevent this, they had to pump inert argon gas into the silo to smother any fire. Now nuclear scientists and engineers are faced with dealing with this problem. They hope to use robots which can swim and operate in the dark to locate and classify the material. However, this will not be easy. When the radioactive waste is classified, the scientists will

9. Robin McKie, 'The Most Dangerous Place in Europe,' *The Observer*, 19 April 2009, p. 20.
10. Ibid.

attempt to mix the radioactive waste with liquid glass and allow the glass to harden. This process is called vitrification. While it may sound easy, there are multiple stages in the process where radioactive contamination could take place. Cleaning up a single building will take ten years because everything has to be done slowly and carefully to avoid leaks. There are so many potential pitfalls that one of the senior employees at Sellafield told McKie that, 'if you want to object to anything nuclear, you have just to point to Sellafield.'[11]

In 2006, UK government inspectors raised serious questions about the safety of some other ageing nuclear power plants in Britain. These included the deterioration of reactor cores in Hinkley Point B in Somerset. Documents obtained under Freedom of Information requests, show that British Energy, the company which operates the nuclear power plants, does not know either the extent of the damage to the reactor cores or why the deterioration has occurred in the first place.[12] The nuclear power plants, which were identified as having problems, include Hinkley Point in Somerset, Hartlepool in Cleveland, Hunterston B in Ayrshire, Heysham 1 in Lancashire, Dungeness in Kent and Torness in East Lothian. John Large, an independent nuclear engineer, who has advised both the government and Greenpeace on the safety of nuclear installations, stated that the government 'was gambling with public safety' to allow Hinkley Point to continue operating.[13]

The Guardian reported on 21 April 2011, that there had been two spillages of radioactive waste in the first three months of 2011. Radioactive material, five times the legal permitted level, leaked from an old ventilation duct at the Sellafield nuclear complex in Cumbria.[14] At Torness nuclear power plant near Edinburgh in Scotland, ground water contaminated with radioactive tritium leaked from two pipelines. Further south at the nuclear power

11. Ibid., p. 21.
12. John Vidal and Ian Sample, 'Documents reveal hidden fears over Britain's nuclear plants,' *The Guardian*, 5 July 2006, p. 1.
13. Ibid., p. 2.
14. Rob Edwards, 'Leaked nuclear reports reveals three incidents at British plants,' *The Guardian*, 21 April 2011, p. 13.

plant in Hartlepool in England, the back-up cooling system malfunctioned because of a faulty valve.

Similar complaints were being made by the Nuclear Installations Inspectorate (NII) in 2009. The NII told the Nuclear Management Partners, the consortium which runs Sellafield, that the possibility of having a serious accident at the plant is still 'far too high'.[15] The Scottish Environmental Protection Agency (Sepa), admitted in September 2011, that radioactive material had leaked for more than two decades at the nuclear power plant at Dounreay. Sepa revealed that it will be impossible to return the seabed in the area to its 'pristine condition'.[16] Tens of thousands of radioactive fuel particles escaped from the nuclear plant between 1963 and 1984. Local beaches were contaminated and fishing in a two-kilometre radius around the plant has been banned since 1997. Experts consider that some of the radioactive particles would be lethal if they were ingested. These particles are about the same size as a grain of sand. They contain caesium-137 which has a half-life of thirty years. Much more worrying is the fact that there are traces of plutonium-239 in the seabed. This has a half-life of 24,000 years. During a hearing at the Wick sheriff court in 2007, the UK Atomic Energy Authority which operated the power station at the time, pleaded guilty to the charge that 'they failed to prevent fragments of irradiated nuclear fuel being discharged into the environment.' The operators were fined £140.000.[17] The scale of the contamination is enormous. 2,300 radioactive particles have been recovered since 2008. In the summer of 2011, three hundred and fifty one particles were discovered and removed by an underwater vehicle. Since 1983, four hundred and eighty radioactive particles have been found on three beaches in the area.

A document written by Britain's chief nuclear inspector, Mike Weightman, obtained by *The Observer* under the Freedom of Information Act, revealed that there had been more than 1,750

---

15. Terry MacAlister, 'Crumbling stores, leaky plants and dangers of old age,' *The Guardian*, 21 October 2009, p. 12.
16. Rob Edwards, 'Dounreay seabed can never be radiation free,' *The Guardian*, 22 September 2011, p. 8.
17. Ibid.

leaks, breakdowns or other incidents at nuclear power plants across Britain during the previous seven years.[18]

The report revealed that the British government's approach to nuclear safety regulation is different from many other countries which have nuclear energy. The Nuclear Installation Inspectorate (NII) does not employ sufficient numbers of staff to set regulations with which the industry can comply. The NII sets general targets for the industry to reduce risks as low as is reasonably practical, and then regulates the industry through issuing licences with strict safety conditions attached.[19]

Environmental organisations such as Greenpeace find this practice unacceptable. But other independent voices are also critical of this way of dealing with the nuclear industry. According to John Lange, an independent nuclear engineer, 'Britain's nuclear inspectors are facing serious problems with serious implications. Some of these incidents were potentially disastrous. We already have evidence that their staffing crisis is compromising their regulation of nuclear safety. Without a strong and effective regulator, the risk of a large release of radioactivity increases.'[20]

British Government Attempted to Downplay the Seriousness of the Accident at Fukushima

On 1 July 2011, *The Guardian* revealed that the British government attempted to cover-up the seriousness of the accident at Fukushima. 'British government officials approached nuclear companies to draw up a coordinated public relations strategy to play down the Fukushima nuclear accident just two days after the earthquake and tsunami in Japan and before the extent of the radiation leak was known.'[21] Journalists from *The Guardian* got access to emails between key government departments, which show that government officials were working behind the scenes

18. Terry MacAlister and Rob Edwards, 'In a secret health and safety report, the chief nuclear inspector admits Britain's watchdog force is short of experienced staff,' *The Observer*, 21 June, 2009.
19. Ibid.
20. Ibid.
21. Rob Edwards, 'UK bid to play down Japan crisis revealed: PR drive two days after Fukushima to shore up British nuclear ambitions,' *The Guardian*, 1 July 2011, p. 1.

with the multinational companies EDF Energy, Areva and Westinghouse, to try to ensure that the coverage which was given to what was happening at Fukushima would not derail the government plan to build new nuclear power stations. One official at the Department of Business, Innovation and Skills (BIS), whose name was concealed, wrote that, 'this has the potential to set the nuclear industry back globally.'[22] In a folksy, inclusive but very authoritarian tone he wrote, 'we need to ensure that the anti-nuclear chaps and chapesses do not gain ground on this. We need to occupy the territory and hold it. We really need to show the safety of nuclear.'[23]

The Soviet Union Nuclear Accident

The accident at Chernobyl on 26 April 1986, hurled 190 tonnes of uranium and graphite into the atmosphere. This radioactive material, the equivalent of 400 Hiroshima bombs, was carried by the wind, all over western Europe and contaminated an area of 150,000 square miles. The cloud reached Ireland two days later, bringing with it radioactive elements such as iodine-131, caesium-137, caesium-134, ruthenium-103, and ruthenium-106. When it rained that weekend, the levels of caesium-137 increased forty-fold. Sheep from upland areas of Donegal and Mayo are still regularly tested for radiation.

The Soviet authorities tried to cover up the incident. Many believe that in the intervening years there has been an attempt to downgrade the catastrophe. A World Health Organisation (WHO) report in 2005, estimated that only fifty people had died but that another 9,000 may die in the future as a result of being exposed to radiation.[24]

Helen Caldicott, author of *Nuclear is Not the Answer*, disputes the WHO figures.[25] She quotes a 2009 report, published by the New York Academy of Sciences entitled, 'Chernobyl: Consequences of the Catastrophe for People and the Environment.' The three

22. Ibid.
23. Ibid.
24. Karen Charman, 'Brave Nuclear World?' *World-Watch*, July / August 2006, p. 12.
25. Helen Caldicott, *Nuclear Power is Not the Answer*, The New Press, London, 2006, pp. 74–80.

scientist authors – Alexey V. Yablokov, Vassily B. Nesterenko, and Alexey V. Nesterenko – provide in its pages a translated synthesis and compilation of hundreds of scientific articles which appeared in Slavic publications over the past twenty years. The articles analyse the effects of the Chernobyl disaster on people and the environment. They estimate the number of deaths attributable to the Chernobyl meltdown at about 980,000.[26] Caldicott goes on to question the competence of the WHO findings, because of its close relationship with the International Atomic Energy Agency (IAEA). According to her, 'In the early days of nuclear power, WHO issued forthright statements on radiation risks such as its 1956 warning: 'Genetic heritage is the most precious property for human beings. It determines the lives of our progeny, health and harmonious development of future generations. As experts, we affirm that the health of future generations is threatened by increasing development of the atomic industry and sources of radiation ... We also believe that new mutations that occur in humans are harmful to them and their offspring.'[27]

After 1959, the WHO did not make any further statement on the relationship between health and radioactivity. What happened? On 28 May 1959, at the 12th World Health Assembly, the WHO drew up an agreement with the IAEA. Clause 12.40 of this agreement says: 'Whenever either organisation [the WHO or the IAEA] proposes to initiate a programme or activity on a subject in which the other organisation has or may have a substantial interest, the first party shall consult the other with a view to adjusting the matter by mutual agreement.'[28] She goes on to quote Dr Michael Fernex who worked for the WHO and was formerly an academic at the University of Basel. She quotes him as saying in 2004 that, 'Six years ago we tried to have a conference. The proceedings were never published. This is because in this matter the organisations at the UN are subordinate to the IAEA ... Since

---

26. Helen Caldicott, 'How nuclear apologists mislead the world over radiation,' *The Guardian*, 11 April 2011, http://www.guardian.co.uk/environment/2011/04/11/nuclear-apologists-radiation.
27. Ibid.
28. Helen Caldicott, 2005, *Nuclear Power is Not the Answer*, The New Press, London, p. 75.

1986, the WHO did nothing about studying Chernobyl. The interdiction to publish came from the IAEA. The IAEA blocked the proceedings; the truth would have been a disaster for the nuclear industry.'[29]

Those most at risk at Chernobyl were the 650,000 soldiers known as 'liquidators' who were brought in from all over the Soviet Union to put out the fire and deal with the aftermath of the nuclear explosion. Their work involved demolishing villages, dumping high levels of radioactive waste, cleaning railway lines and roads, and decontaminating the environment. Many of these men developed terminal cancer, but since they had returned to their communities they were seldom counted among the casualties of Chernobyl.[30] Konstantin Tatuyan, one of the 'liquidators' at Chernobyl, told John Vidal of *The Guardian*, that, 'nearly all his colleagues had died or had cancer of one sort or another, but no one ever asked him for evidence. There was burning resentment at the way the UN, the industry and ill-informed pundits had played down the catastrophe.'[31] Vidal tells those who are of the opinion that only fifty people were killed at Chernobyl to go and speak to doctors and those who dealt directly with the catastrophe.[32]

In 2011, what is left at Chernobyl of reactor No. 4, continues to burn under the concrete and steel sarcophagus which was built hastily after 1986. This structure is now disintegrating. There is a plan to build a replacement and slide it over the present sarcophagus. The new cover will be the size of a soccer pitch and taller than the Statue of Liberty. It will be the largest moveable structure ever built.[33]

David Marples, a historian and expert on Chernobyl, also challenges the findings of the UN Chernobyl Report. He states that in the city of Gomel, which is less than eighty kilometres from Chernobyl, the documentary film *Chernobyl Hearts* had claimed

29. Ibid.
30. John Vidal, 'Hell on Earth,' *The Guardian, Society/Guardian/ Environment*, 26 April 2006, p. 9.
31. John Vidal, 'Nuclear's green cheerleaders forget Chernobyl at our peril,' *The Guardian*, 2 April 2011, p. 38.
32. Ibid.
33. Richard Stone, 'The Long Shadow of Chernobyl,' *National Geographic*, April 2006, pp. 36, 50.

that the incidence of thyroid cancer is 10,000 times higher than before the accident. The website Chernobyl 1, claims that congenital birth defects have increased by 250 per cent since the accident, and infant mortality is 300 times higher than in the rest of Europe.[34]

In Ukraine and Belarus, huge tracts of fertile land have been contaminated and will not be able to produce food for thousands of years. It is estimated that 150,000 square kilometres, an area about the size of Denmark, was contaminated. More than 400,000 people were removed from the area and, as happened in the area around Fukushima, will not be able to return for decades. Their lives have been ruined.

But the fallout from the accident reached much further than the surrounding countries. In Britain, about 1,500 miles from the destroyed reactor, twenty-six years after the accident, 382 farms containing over one quarter of a million sheep are still affected by high levels of caesium-137 in their meat. These animals have to be moved to other areas, less affected by the radioactive contamination, before they are sold.[35]

Caldicott also points to health problems caused by the accident at Chernobyl. Between 1986 and 2001, 8,353 cases of thyroid cancer occurred, 716 of these were children, 342 were adolescents and 7,300 were adults. Many have had their thyroid gland removed, so they are now dependent on thyroxin replacement tablets to survive.

USA Nuclear Accident

At 4 a.m. on 28 March 1979, a meltdown happened at the Three Mile Island (TMI) nuclear power plant in Pennsylvania. According to Dr Helen Caldicott, it began with a mechanical failure which was followed by an automatic shutdown in the secondary coolant system which, in turn, closed some valves. This caused the water in the primary coolant system to overheat and become ineffective. As a result, the one hundred tonnes of uranium in the reactor core began to overheat and melt.[36] For the duration

34. Karen Charman, 'Brave Nuclear World?,' World-Watch, July / August 2006, pp. 12–13.
35. Helen Caldicott, op. cit., pp. 65–74.
36. Ibid.

of the accident, highly radioactive cooling water continued to be pumped through a valve onto the floor of the reactor and from there into a tank in an adjacent building, where large quantities of radioactive gas was being released into the atmosphere. Caldicott goes on to accuse both the industry and the government of failing to provide any accurate data on the 'specific isotopes [which] escaped nor the actual quantity of the radiation that was released'.[37] The collusion between the nuclear industry and the regulator is most evident in the refusal to agree to a request from a radiation expert, Dr Carl Johnson, to conduct a survey to look for these radioactive elements in the dust around Three Mile Island after the accident. She also claims that, in the years following the accident, there has been 'a deficit of studies performed on the medical outcomes of this accident and a plethora of studies relating peoples' symptoms to stress'.[38] Furthermore, 'the official health studies were paid for by TMI Public Health Fund, which was set up by the nuclear industry and funded by industry payments, which also settled property damage suits. At no stage did the nuclear industry confer with or obtain evidence from citizens who believed that they had been impacted by the accident.'[39]

Writing in *The New York Times*, on the first anniversary of the accident at Fukushima, Kristen Iversen linked the misinformation about the seriousness of the Fukushima accident with her own growing up in Arvada, Colorado, in the United States. A factory in Rocky Flats produced plutonium 'triggers' for the US arsenal of nuclear weapons between 1952 and 1989. No one was really sure what was being produced at the factory. No one was told about the 'two large fires, in 1957 and 1969, that sent radioactive plumes over the Denver metro area. Wind and water carried radioactive elements into the surrounding neighbourhoods, including mine.'[40] She goes on to write about the bravery of one man who pursued the issue and was eventually fired. 'One man tried to

---

37. Ibid. p. 66.
38. Ibid. p. 71.
39. Ibid. p. 72.
40. Kristen Iversen, 'Nuclear Fallout,' *The New York Times*, 10 March 2012, http://www.nytimes.com/2012/03/11/opinion/sunday/fallout-at-a-former-nuclear-weapon-plant.html.

sound the alarm. Dr Carl Johnson, Jefferson County health director from 1973 to 1981, directed numerous studies on contamination levels and health risks which the plant posed to public health. Based on his conclusions, Dr Johnson opposed housing development near Rocky Flats. He was fired. Later studies confirmed many of his findings.'[41] Further on in the article she writes, 'In spite of everything we've learned, profit continues to trump safety.'[42]

According to the Union of Concerned Scientists (UCS) Report, these 'legacy subsidies' are seven cents per kilowatt-hour. This is the equivalent of about 140 per cent of the average wholesale price of power in the years between 1960 and 2008. This makes the subsidy more valuable than the power produced by nuclear power plants during these years. Without these subsidies, the nuclear industry would not have been able to build and run nuclear power plants, unless they charged their customers higher prices for their electricity. The authors of the USC report claim that 'the nuclear industry is only able to portray itself as a low-cost power supplier today because of past government subsidies and write-offs.'

---

41. Ibid.
42. Ibid.

CHAPTER SIX

The Real Cost of Nuclear Power

One month before the disaster at the nuclear power plant at Fukushima, the Union of Concerned Scientists (UCS) in the United States published a paper on the economics of nuclear power. The study points out that subsidies to the nuclear power industry in the past fifty years in the United States have been so large in proportion to the value of the energy produced that, in some cases, it would have cost the taxpayer less to simply buy kilowatts on the open market and give them away.[1] The study states that while the exact value of the subsidies, which the nuclear industry has received is difficult to ascertain, even a conservative estimate results in a very high figure. In some situations, it adds up almost to the value of the power that nuclear power plants produce. Sometimes, this is close to one hundred per cent, or even higher, when 'legacy' subsidies are included.

Originally, the subsidies were designed to provide temporary cover for the fledgling nuclear industry. In 1954, the utility company, General Electric, ran an advertisement which stated that, 'in five years – certainly within ten, civilian reactors would be "privately" financed and built without government subsidy.' The subsidies are still in place in 2012. The high subsidies allow the nuclear industry to exaggerate the competitiveness of nuclear-produced power in comparison to less risky alternatives such as promoting energy efficiency and renewable forms of energy.[2]

People often think that government subsidies given to failing companies come as cash grants. This is not what happens in the nuclear industry. Rather, subsidies are used to move construction costs and liability from operating risks from the shoulders of the investor to the taxpayer. The taxpayers are 'burdened with an array of risks, ranging from cost overruns and defaults to

---

1. 'Nuclear Power Subsidies: The Gift that Keeps on Taking,' http://www.uc-susa.org/nuclear_power/nuclear_power_and_global_warming/nuclear-power-subsidies-report.html.
2. Ibid.

accidents and nuclear waste management'.[3] In practice, this means that the companies which own and run the nuclear reactors 'have never been economically responsible for the full costs and risks of their operations'.[4] These subsidies have allowed utility companies to offset their capital costs in building the reactors. This has often been done through investment tax credits and accelerated depreciation of the plant. Utility companies are allowed to depreciate new reactors over a fifteen year period, instead of over the forty to sixty years during which the plant is expected to operate. According to the UCS Report, this tax break equals between $40 and $80 million per annum at the 2011 construction cost estimates.

Loan guarantees have also been made available to utility companies to allow them to borrow money at a very low rate of interest. This is made possible by municipal bonds and Build America Bonds. Many states in the US allow utility companies to charge ratepayers for Construction Work in Progress (CWIP) by including a surcharge in the bills they send out to their customers. Once again, this moves the cost of construction away from the company onto the shoulders of the consumer. To a lesser extent, subsidies have been made available to buy land on which the reactor will be built.

Similar offsets are available to buy uranium. This may seem strange as the cost of uranium is relatively low. But the subsidies also cover both mining and enrichment operations which are very expensive. In mining, for example, 'the industry continues to receive a special depletion allowance for uranium mining, equal to twenty-two per cent of the ore's market value, and its deductions are allowed to exceed the gross investment in a given mine.'[5] Furthermore, a Mining Act dating back to 1872, governs the mining of uranium on public lands. The companies do not have to pay royalties to the government for extracting such ore. The awful consequences, from an ecological perspective, is that the

3. 'Nuclear Power Still Not Viable without Subsidies,' Union of Concerned Scientists report, 23 February 2011.
4. Ibid., p. 6.
5. Ibid., p. 7.

remediation costs for many of the 4,000 mines from which uranium has been taken in the past, exceeds the market value of all the ore which has been extracted. The cost of remediation is not levied on the company. Rather, it falls to the taxpayer.

Enriching uranium involves turning uranium into fuel for the nuclear reactors. Enrichment facilities have also benefited from subsidies and Federal loans. The US Congress agreed to $2 billion in loan guarantees to build new enrichment facilities in the US. This has been topped up with a similar amount from the Department of Energy.[6]

Subsidies were also designed to shift the long-term risks to the public. The main vehicle which facilitated this was the Price-Anderson Act which put a cap on the nuclear industry's liability for third-party damage to people and property.[7] The Union of Concerned Scientists' Report makes the point that security concerns have escalated considerably since the events of 11 September 2001. The Report states that 'the complexity and lack of data in these areas made it impossible to quantify the magnitude of security subsidies for this analysis. But it is clear that as the magnitude of the threat increases, taxpayers will be forced to bear a greater share of risks.'[8] The Price-Anderson Act requires utility companies to carry a preset amount of insurance for offsite damage caused by an accident at a nuclear power plant. The companies are required to contribute to a fund to cover a preset portion of the damages. However, the main focus of the Act is to limit liability to the utility companies at a 'much lower (level) than would be needed in a variety of plausible accident scenarios'.[9]

Britain

As happened in the US, the British government made huge financial contributions to the nuclear industry, through subsidies and the availability of cheap credit. As late as 2002, the government came to the rescue of British Energy with a £650 million credit

6. Ibid., p. 8.
7. Ibid., p. 8.
8. Ibid., p. 8.
9. Ibid., p. 9.

facility. The New Economics Foundation (NEF), which was founded in 1994, is an innovative think-and-do-tank that inspires and delivers real economic well-being through improving the quality of the lives of people by promoting innovative solutions. It often challenges mainstream thinking on social, economic and ecological issues. A report from NEF entitled 'Mirage and Oasis: Energy Choices in an Age of Global Warming' published in Britain in 2005, concluded that the cost of building new nuclear power plants in the United Kingdom has been underestimated by a factor of three. It also debunked the claim that nuclear power is a timely response to global warming and climate change. Nuclear power takes too long to come on stream. A British government review in 2002 estimated that it would take a minimum of twenty years to develop a nuclear power programme based on the Westinghouse Advanced Passive 1000 (AP1000).[10]

The NEF study concluded that nuclear energy is too expensive and, in the age of terrorist threats, a security risk. Nuclear power also leaves a toxic legacy.[11] Finally, it stated that 'against every meaningful criteria, whether to do with cost, security, or environmental friendliness; with flexibility; or with the potential for a guaranteed long-term supply and job creation, the appropriate renewable energy source wins every time.'[12]

In her book *Nuclear Power is not the Answer*, Helen Caldicott, lists a number of subsidies which the British government has given to the nuclear industry. 'In 1989, the British government withdrew nuclear power from its electricity sector privatisation programme because it was seen to be too great an investment risk.'[13] One year later, a consumer subsidy, equal to fifty per cent of the government-owned Nuclear Electric's income in 1990, was introduced to prop-up the ailing nuclear sector. At that point, the nuclear utility could recover only half of its costs from the sale of its electricity to the new electricity market.

10. 'Mirage and oasis: Energy choices in an age of global warming,' a Report from the New Economic Foundation, June 2005.
11. Ibid.
12. Ibid., p. 5.
13. Helen Caldicott, Nuclear Power is Not the Answer, *The New Press*, New York, 2005, p. 31.

Nuclear Power is not Cheap

The last British nuclear power station, Sizewell B, was built in Suffolk in 1995. The price paid by the taxpayer then was £2.73 billion which would translate into £3.9 billion in 2008 figures. It took fifteen years to complete and it cost twice the original budget. If commercial companies had built the plant, the cost of borrowing the money would have pushed the total amount to well over the £4 billion mark. It would take more than six similar nuclear power plants to supply twenty per cent of Britain's electricity. Both land-based and offshore wind farms would supply the same amount of energy for a similar cost of around £25 billion according to Dr Dave Toke.[14]At that point, the cost bias moves in favour of wind energy, as fuel costs are free and decommissioning is far less expensive. Walt Patterson, an Associate Fellow in the Energy, Environment and Development programme at Chatham House, makes the point that in tackling climate change or insuring security of supply, nuclear energy is the, 'slowest, most expensive, least flexible and riskiest option'.[15] If it were not for hidden subsidies, especially from the military, the economics of nuclear power would look worse.

The former Environment Minister, Michael Meacher, believes that, given the costs and the risks, the private sector will not invest in nuclear facilities unless the government underwrites the loans and provides tax relief for the industry.[16] This is precisely what the Brown government planned to do when the then Energy and Climate Secretary, Ed Miliband, identified ten possible sites for nuclear power stations in November 2009.[17] This may be difficult to accomplish in the present British, European and global economic climate. For example, Adris Piebalgs, the then commissioner for energy in the European Commission, wanted to see different forms of energy compete against each other on a level playing

14. Dave Toke, 'Doubters: It strains the logic of energy,' *The Guardian*, Society/Guardian /Environment, 5 October 2005, p. 9.

15. Walt Patterson, 'Time for an upgrade,' *The Guardian*, Society/Guardian /Environment, 17 May 2006, p. 8.

16. David Toke, op. cit.

17. David Teather, 'Ten to follow: UK's nuclear future is mapped out as race to tackle climate change hots up,' *The Guardian*, 10 November 2009, p. 4.

field. He will not countenance the use of state funds to subsidise nuclear power.[18]

Despite the then Labour government's attempt to put nuclear power back on the agenda, many people believe that economic arguments will scuttle the proposal. According to Tom Burke, a visiting professor at both Imperial College, London and University College London, 'nuclear power stations are financially-risky projects. You spend hundreds of millions of pounds for at least a decade before you start to recover any earnings. Since you have to pay for the financing as well as the direct construction costs, this makes nuclear power much less attractive to investors than any other form of electricity generation.'[19] The only way to make the nuclear option palatable to investors is to push up the price of electricity. The public will hardly tolerate such an action.

More Powerful Seismic Activity in the Past Decade Makes Nuclear Power more Expensive
On 26 December 2004, the Simeule earthquake close to Indonesia, registered 9.1 on the Richter scale. The tsunami which it unleashed across the Indian Ocean killed 230,000 people in fourteen countries and destroyed the lives of tens of thousands more. Quakes of such magnitude are not confined to Asia. On 27 Feb 2010, an earthquake of 8.8 magnitude, one of the largest ever recorded, tore apart houses, bridges and highways in central Chile and sent a tsunami racing halfway around the world. Building nuclear power plants in a part of the world which is seismically unpredictable, is clearly irresponsible.

Demands for more stringent safety standards at nuclear power installations will reach far beyond the shores of Japan. The International Atomic Energy Agency (IAEA) states that 88 of the current 442 nuclear installations worldwide are located in areas of high seismic activity.[20] In the opinion of John Vidal of *The Guardian*,

---

18. Michael Brooks 'Is it all over for nuclear power?,' *New Scientist*, 22 April 2006, p. 36.
19. Tom Burke, 'Nuclear industry will only build stations the prime minister wants if he forces up electricity prices,' *The Guardian*, 18 May 2006, p. 34.
20. Paul Marks, 'Seismic zones share out nuclear problems,' *NewScientist*, 19 March 2011, p. 8.

the figure is closer to 100.[21] One can expect that, from 2012 onwards, politicians and regulators will come under pressure to decommission many of these dangerous power stations. John Stevenson of the IAEA's International Seismic Centre says that, 'the nuclear regulatory agencies will want to re-examine the potential for tsunami risks on the Pacific Rim and possibly the other oceans as well.'[22]

The earthquake that hit the East Coast of the US on 23 August 2011 registered 5.8 on the Richter scale. It caused the North Anna nuclear power plant to shut down. This has raised serious questions about whether some US nuclear power plants are earthquake-proof. The Nuclear Regulatory Commission is so concerned about the situation that it has assigned a special team to study the earthquake's effect on North Anna. The findings will have serious implications for all the nuclear reactors in the eastern United States, many of which were not built with this magnitude of an earthquake in mind.[23] The article calls attention to the lack of honesty in the nuclear industry which, unfortunately, is a recurring theme in this book. In 1973, when the company at the North Anna plant was digging the foundations for the third reactor at the site, a visiting geology professor told an executive from Virginia Electric & Power Company, that there was a geologic fault in the area. The executive, whether intentionally or not, neglected the geologist's advice and the company told the Nuclear Regulatory Commission that there was no evidence of faults. The company paid a fine of $32,000 for failing to alert the regulators.[24] Such a small fine for something which could have been so serious, does not inspire much confidence in the regulator.

21. John Vidal, 'Japan's avoidable accidents make folly of nuclear energy clear,' The Irish Times, 15 March 2011, p. 15.
22. Paul Marks, op.cit., p. 8.
23. Matthew L. Lald, 'After Quake, Virginia Nuclear Plant Takes Stock,' The New York Times, 8 September 2011, http://www.nytimes.com/2011/09/08/science/earth/08nuclear.html.
24. Ibid.

Time Constraints

If economics is undermining the viability of building new nuclear power stations, then the time it takes to build a nuclear power station may be a further nail in the coffin of the industry. There is simply not the capacity to start a massive nuclear building programme in Britain or anywhere around the world. In October 2005, Ian Fells, a British energy consultant, told an energy conference at Rimini in Italy that there are only six building companies in the world capable of building nuclear power stations. None of these companies is British and the specialised personnel who built the last British nuclear plant, Sizewell B, are either retired or dead. Even to retain the present nuclear status quo in Britain, would require the building of eight to ten nuclear power stations with little hope of their being completed and operational before 2025. The reality is that, even before Fukushima, nuclear power was on the decline. As of 1 April 2011, there were seven fewer reactors in the world than in 2002.[25] Over the past decade, the role which nuclear power has played in supplying energy is contracting. It is now responsible for about fourteen per cent of the world's electricity. More worrying, the average life of nuclear power plants is twenty-six years, which means that, in a post-Fukushima world, these plants will continue to operate for another decade and a half which many scientists consider to be risky.

Civilian and Military Nuclear Power are Siamese Twins

Another major cost is the increased militarisation of our contemporary world. I have already quoted the words of the Swedish Nobel prize winning physicist, Hannes Alven, who said that the peaceful atom and military atom are 'Siamese twins'. The primary purpose of the first nuclear power plant built at Calder Hall (at Sellafield) in 1955, was to produce plutonium for atom bombs.

---

25. Mycle Schneider, Atony Froggatt, Steve Thomas, 'The World Nuclear Industry Status Report 2010-2011, Nuclear Power in a Post Fukushima World,' WorldWatch Institute, Washington DC, April 2011, http://www.worldwatch.org/nuclear-power-after-fukushima.

The Oxford Research Group came to the same conclusions. In a paper published in 2006 entitled, 'Global Responses to Global Threats: Sustainable Security for the 21st Century,' Paul Rogers and John Sloboda wrote, 'civilian nuclear activities and nuclear weapons proliferation are intimately linked; one of the twins cannot be promoted without the other spreading out of control.'[26]

Currently, about sixty countries in the world have civilian nuclear power plants. It is estimated that over the past forty years, twenty of these countries have used their supposedly civilian nuclear facilities to undertake covert research on a weapons programme.

In Japan in 2002, the Chief Cabinet Secretary, Yasu Kukuda, became the most senior official in Tokyo to leave the door open for Japan to develop its own nuclear weapons. He was reflecting on the fact that India, China and North Korea possessed nuclear weapons and that, in the future, Japan may not be able to rely on the nuclear umbrella which the US currently provides for Japan.[27]

In August 2011, the *NewScientist* reported that the use of laser power will make it very difficult to know whether the enriched uranium is destined for nuclear power stations or bombs. General Electric and Hitachi are about to build a laser facility in Wilmington, North Carolina, which will produce 1,000 tonnes of enriched fuel every year. There are two benefits from this laser enrichment process. Firstly, it is more efficient and, secondly, it does not use as much power as the current process. The down-side, according to the article, is 'that rogue states could find it easier to make atom-bomb fuel in secret, as smaller facilities are needed for this method, making it impossible to detect using satellite imagery.'[28]

26. Chris Abbot, Paul Rogers and John Sloboda, 2006, 'Global Responses to Global Threats for the 21st Century,' Oxford Research Group, p. 10, http://www.scribd.com /doc/2588201/Global-Responses-to-Global-Threats-Sustainable-Security-for-the-21st-Century.

27. Robyn Lim, 'So much for Japan's nuclear taboo,' *Herald-Tribune*, 13 June 2012, p. 8.

28. *NewScientist*, 27 August 2011, p. 4.

Fires

Fires also pose threats to nuclear installations. In June 2011, fires burned to within a few miles of a dump site near Los Alamos where scientists connected with the Manhattan Project had developed the atomic bomb during the Second World War. The dump contained 20,000 barrels of plutonium-contaminated waste which included contaminated clothes and equipment. The director of operations at the laboratory assured the public that there was no immediate threat to public safety 'even in extreme conditions.'

CHAPTER SEVEN

Nuclear Waste

Nuclear Fission is an Inherently Dangerous Industry
In 2011, nuclear reactors generated about fourteen per cent of the world's electricity. At the same time, reactors generated 12,000 tonnes of waste each year. Some of this waste will remain dangerously radioactive for thousands of years.[1]

As far back as 1984, in the wake of the nuclear accident at Three Mile Island, Charles Perrow, the author of the book, *Normal Accidents: Living with High-Risk Technologies,* analysed the potential for accidents when complex technologies are operating.[2] He concluded his reflections on Three Mile Island with the words, 'no matter how effective conventional safety devices are, there is a form of accident that is inevitable,' hence, 'normal accidents'. He compares a pile-up on a motorway with a nuclear accident and noted that while a motorway crash is disastrous for those involved, it cannot be described as a disaster. The latter only happens when the technologies involved have the potential to affect large numbers of innocent bystanders, not just today, but into the indefinite future. In discussing the morality of civilian nuclear power, the inherent catastrophic potential of this technology is the primary moral principle. Fintan O'Toole, a columnist in *The Irish Times,* argued that nuclear technology, with multiple inherent dangers, is a classic example of human hubris. He wrote, 'The engineers who design nuclear plants know very well that the consequences of a systems failure may be catastrophic. They also know that creating waste which will remain toxic for 100,000 years is a horizon of time far beyond the imaginative capacity of the human mind. However, they keep this knowledge at bay. They believe that the consequences are irrelevant because the system will not fail.'[3] In the view of Dr William Reville, a senior

---

1. *NewScientist,* 16 October 2010, p. 38.
2. Charles Perrow, *Normal Accidents: Living with High-Risk Technologies,* Basic Books, NY, 1984.
3. Fintan O'Toole, 'Enticed by long-odds Fukushima gamble,' *The Irish Times,* 22 March 2011, p. 16.

lecturer in biochemistry in University College Cork, and a regular contributor to *The Irish Times*, 'nuclear fission is a failed technology. It generates waste that must be segregated from the environment for 100,000 years. It offers governments a cheap way to develop nuclear weapons; nuclear power stations are built on the open surfaces of the earth and are very vulnerable to terrorist attack and to bombing in conventional warfare. The industry should be phased out.'[4]

At every stage of the nuclear journey there is a serious problem with waste. The further one moves along the journey, the more toxic and carcinogenic the waste becomes. Eighty-five per cent of the waste used in the enrichment process is known as depleted uranium. This has to be placed in sealed containers and safely stored in a stable geological site. In the US alone, there are now more than 500,000 tonnes of depleted uranium. The main storage problem is with plutonium because its half-life, which is the time it takes to lose half of its radioactivity, is 24,000 years, and even minute amounts can cause cancer. Hence, plutonium waste will have to be guarded for tens of thousands of years and this will place an extraordinary burden on future generations. A fundamental, ethical principle called intergenerational justice, states that people living in one generation should not saddle future generations with a burden such as plutonium waste.

An incredible 103 tonnes of plutonium is stored at Sellafield.[5] In September 2007, a report from the Royal Society of London, written by Professor Geoffrey Boulton, stated that the plutonium stockpile at Sellafield might be vulnerable to terrorist attack. He recommended that the UK government needs to find a way to use or dispose of this material.[6]

Nuclear waste is not confined to what is produced in the nuclear reactors. Mining uranium has very significant negative environmental consequences. The Olympic Dam uranium/copper

---

4. Dr William Reville, 'Science in a world of anxiety,' *The Irish Times*, 1 November 2001, p. 8.
5. David Adams, 'Sellafield's plutonium store "vulnerable to terrorist attack",' *The Guardian*, 21 September 2007, http://www.guardian.co.uk/uk/2007/sep/21/politics.terrorism/print. Downloaded on 31 March 2011.
6. Ibid.

mine, in South Australia, has produced sixty million tonnes of radioactive tailings and the amount is increasing at ten million tonnes each year.

Most commercially-viable deposits of uranium are found in Australia, Canada, South Africa, Russia, US and Uzbekistan. Typically, 98,000 tonnes of rock has to be mined and milled in order to produce a single tonne of uranium. The tailings from the milling, much of which contains uranium, must be secured. This seldom happens. In the 1980s, material which contained highly-radioactive tailings was used to build houses.[7]

There are also major problems with water extraction because, for example, in South Australia, a uranium mine sucks more than thirty million litres of water from the Great Artesian Basin. It is impossible to quantify the full environmental cost of the operation since this mine has secured a range of exemptions from environmental legislation. For example, it is exempt from the South Australian Environmental Protection Act, The Water Resources Act, The Aboriginal Heritage Act and The Freedom of Information Act.[8] Little wonder then that in 2003, the Australian Senate's Inquiry into the regulation of uranium mining in Australia found 'a pattern of underperformance and non-compliance.'[9] The mine is also the largest consumer of electricity in South Australia, making it the State's major contributor to global warming.

Milling uranium uses huge diesel-powered machines to crush the rock. Then sulphuric acid is used to leach the uranium from the rock. Other elements are also leached, among them selenium, arsenic and lead. These are then removed before the fully milled product is completed.

Beyond milling, there is the process of enrichment which is not unlike distillation. Gases used in this process, such as fluorine and

---

7. Jon Hughes, ibid., p. 45.
8. Australian Conservation Foundation, 2005, 'Submission to Standing Committee on Industry and Resources, Inquiry into Developing Australia' Non-fossil Fuel EnergyIndustry. www.aph.gov.au/house/committee/isr/uranium.subs.html.
9. Senate Environment, Communications, Information Technology and the Arts Reference and Legislation Committee, October 2003, 'Regulating the Ranger, Jabiluka, Berverly and Honeymoon uranium mines,' www.aph.gov.au/senate/committee/ecita_ctee/completed_inquiry/2002-04/uranium/report/index.html.

its halogenated compounds have 10,000 times more global warming capacity than carbon dioxide. The nuclear industry does not keep records of the quantity of the various forms of chlorine it releases into the atmosphere.[10] Enriching the uranium also uses enormous amounts of fossil fuel.

For many reasons, which include cost and the opposition of local people, suitable places for the disposal of nuclear waste have not been found thus far. Steve Thomas in his pamphlet, *The Economics of Nuclear Power: An Update*, writes that 'from a moral point of view, the current generation should be extremely wary of leaving such an uncertain, expensive and potentially dangerous legacy to a future generation to deal with when there are no ways of reliably ensuring that the current generation can bequeath the funds to deal with them, much less bear the physical risk.'[11]

Dr Helen Caldicott, the founding president of Physicians for Social Responsibility, is very worried about the dangers to human health from nuclear waste. She points to the longevity of radioactive elements such as strontium-90. This is a tasteless and invisible radioactive element which remains radioactive for six hundred years. The body mistakes strontium-90 for calcium, therefore contaminated milk can enter the body and concentrate in bones and the lactating breasts of women, giving rise to bone cancer, leukaemia and breast cancer. Dr Caldicott is keen to point out that babies and young children are ten to twenty times more susceptible to the carcinogenic effects of radiation than adults.[12] According to Caldicott, plutonium is so carcinogenic that, hypothetically, half a kilo of plutonium evenly distributed around the globe could kill everyone on the planet. Plutonium is dangerous for more than 200,000 years. It enters the body through the lungs and acts like iron. It can then migrate to the bones where it causes bone cancer, or to the liver where it causes liver cancer. Its ability to damage continues into the next generation because it can cross through the placenta into the embryo and cause birth defects.[13]

10. Jon Hughes, 'Conversion and Enrichment,' *The Ecologist*, July-August, 2006, p. 47.
11. Steve Thomas, *The Economics of Nuclear Power: An Update*, Heinrich-Boll-Stiftung European Union, Brussels, p. 17.
12. Dr Helen Caldicott, 'Clean power source should carry a global warning,' *The Sydney Morning Herald*, 27 August 2001, p. 8.
13. Ibid.

The accident at Sellafield was not a once-off event in the history of Britain's nuclear power record. In May 2006, the British government brought a criminal prosecution against British Nuclear Group (BNG), a subsidiary of British Nuclear Fuels, in relation to a major leak at the Thorp reprocessing plant in 2005. Under their licence, the operators of Thorp, which is part of the Sellafield complex, are legally obliged to ensure that radioactive material is properly contained and, if something happens, for example, a major leak, they are required to report the matter to the relevant authorities. In this particular case, 83,000 litres of highly radioactive waste leaked from a pipe into a containment chamber. The waste contained twenty tonnes of uranium and plutonium. It was particularly alarming that staff did not notice the spill for at least eight months! The leak was reported in April 2005, even though it probably began in August 2004. It seems that in March 2008, the staff dismissed the leak as a technical glitch because of the large volume of the spill. An investigation found that there was *operational complacency* among the staff because they believed that leaks of that nature were impossible due to the design of the plant, despite previous evidence to the contrary.[14] Many of Britain's nuclear power plants are reaching the end of their operational life. Fourteen had already been shut down and were in the process of being decommissioned by December 2007.[15]

Factoring in the Cost of Decommissioning

It is very difficult to get a valid cost for decommissioning and dismantling nuclear power plants and disposing safely of the radioactive waste. One reason for this is that, as of 2011, no nuclear power plant anywhere in the world has been decommissioned successfully. The timescale involved in decommissioning could be as long as 150 years, which makes any current projection of the costs involved very difficult to estimate. Nevertheless, the National Audit Office in Britain estimated in January 2008, that

---

14. Liam Reid, 'Sellafield operators sued over major leak at processing plant,' *The Irish Times*, 4 May 2006, p. 8.
15. Colin Brown, 'Nuclear clean-up bill £12bn higher than predicted,' *The Independent*, 30 January 2008, p. 18.

decommissioning Britain's nineteen ageing nuclear power plants would cost the taxpayer £73 billion.[16] This figure came as a surprise as, previously, it had been estimated that the clean-up costs would be more in the region of £61 billion. The reason for the increase is that previous estimates had not included the cost of ponds and silos at Sellafield.[17] Dr Paul Howarth, executive director of Dalton Nuclear Institute at Manchester University, estimates that 'the taxpayer has to pay around £1.5 billion a year to clean-up Sellafield's waste problems and will have to maintain that investment for years to come.'[18]

In July of 2008, The Nuclear Decommissioning Authority (NDA) admitted that the cost of decommissioning could rise even further to £83 billion. The reason given for the increase in cost is the decision to address the complicated hazardous problems at Sellafield, the inflation in the engineering sector of the economy and the lack of income from the Thorp and MOX fuel reprocessing plants.[19] In response to these new figures, Greenpeace's nuclear campaigner, Ben Ayliffe, pointed out that the nuclear clean-up had jumped by £20 billion, and it could even be more expensive as costs spiral out of control.[20]

Still no Permanent Repository for Nuclear Waste

No country, including the US, has made provisions for permanently storing nuclear waste. In 1987 the US Congress had planned to store nuclear waste in a facility at Yucca Mountain in the Nevada desert, about eighty miles north-west of Las Vegas. It came as no surprise that residents and anti-nuclear environmentalists opposed the storing of radioactive material at the site. Nevertheless, the US Congress approved funding for the site in

16. David Hencke, '£73bn to take nuclear plants out of service,' *The Guardian*, 30 January 2008, p. 5.
17. Colin Brown, 'Nuclear clean-up bill £12bn higher than predicted,' *The Independent*, 30 January 2008, p. 18.
18. Robin McKie, 'The Most Dangerous Place In Europe,' *The Observer*, 19 April, 2009, pp. 20–21.
19. Terry Macalister, 'Bill for Britain's nuclear clean-up increases by another £10 billion,' *The Guardian*, 18 July 2008, p. 17.
20. Ibid.

2002. President Obama had promised during his election campaign in 2008 to cancel this project. Accordingly, funding for the site was terminated in 2010 and the licence application was withdrawn in 2011.

A report published in June 2011, by the US Nuclear Regulatory Commission's inspector general, Hubert T. Bell, criticised its chairman Gregory B. Jaczko for using his position to effectively close down the Yucca Mountain site. The report claims that Mr Jaczko used his authority as chairman to carry out the president's wishes while riding roughshod over his fellow commissioners. The inspector claimed that Mr Jaczko failed to fully inform the other four members that he was issuing budget guidelines that would essentially halt the commission's work on the project. It was this commission which would decide whether the Energy Department should be allowed to build and operate the dump (In line with the Obama Administration's policy, the Energy Department had already laid off all the contractors and reassigned its staff).[21]

The report resurrected the long-running battle over how and where to store about 70,000 metric tonnes of the radioactive waste produced by the US's 104 operating nuclear power stations. Proponents of Yucca Mountain, on which about $10 billion has already been spent, say that it provides the safest available disposal of waste that will remain radioactive for thousands of years. The highly-politicised way in which the decision not to proceed with the Yucca Mountain site was made raises serious questions about whether a political agenda takes precedence over safety concerns.

As a result, the US does not have any long-term storage facility for high-level radioactive waste. Commentators point out that, even if all parties agreed on the necessity of reopening the Yucca Mountain site, it would take at least ten years to develop the site to the level where it could begin storing nuclear waste. The nuclear waste mountain continues to rise. The US now has about 72,000

21. John M. Broder and Matthew L. Wald, 'Report Blasts Management Style of Nuclear Regulatory Commission Chairman,' *The New York Times*, 11 June 2011. http://www.nytimes.com/2011/06/11/science/earth/11nuclear.html.

tonnes of spent fuel from civilian reactors and millions of tonnes of nuclear military waste. This is more than the site at Yucca was designed to take.[22]

In Japan, the situation regarding nuclear waste is similar. The Japanese had a plan to send their spent fuel to a reprocessing facility in Rokkasho in the north of Honshu island. After that, they would bury the remainder in a deep repository. Due to political and technical difficulties, this never happened. The Rokkasho facility was originally due to open in 2007 but, because of numerous delays, the date has been postponed many times and may not even open in 2012. As a result, large amounts of spent fuel are being housed in fuel pools around nuclear power stations.

In the *NewScientist*, Allison MacFarlane, associate professor in the Environmental Science and Policy Department at George Mason University in Fairfax, Virginia, asks why so little attention has been given to the nuclear waste issue. MacFarlane has been studying the issue of nuclear energy policy for more than a decade and is a leading expert on nuclear-waste disposal. He recently sat on a National Research Council committee evaluating the US Department of Energy's nuclear-power research and development programs and is chair of the Science and Security Board of the Bulletin of Atomic Scientists.[23] He claims that the nuclear industry is more interested in the 'front end' of the process which involves mining uranium and building power stations and generating electricity because this is where people make money. He maintains that one can see a similar pattern even on a syllabus of nuclear engineering departments in universities. They train plant managers and those who build and design safety issues. Little attention is devoted to the waste issue.[24]

22. Matthew L Wald, 'Japan Nuclear Crisis Revives Long U.S. Flight on Spent Fuel,' *The New York Times*, 23 March 2011, www.nytimes. com/2011/03/24/yucca.html.
23. Media and Public Relations, 'Allison Macfarlane Named to Department of Energy Blue Ribbon Commission on America's Nuclear Future,' 2 February 2010. http://eagle.gmu.edu/newsroom/796/?print.
24. Allison Macfarlane, 'No time to waste,' *NewScientist*, 27 August 2011, pp. 26–7.

Transporting Nuclear Waste

Moving nuclear waste around a country like Britain is another potential area where serious accidents can occur. In fact, there are thirty accidents involving nuclear trains each year in Britain. Some are very serious, but the derailment of a train carrying nuclear waste near the Hinkley Point power station in Somerset in 2003 led Prime Minister Blair to promise a comprehensive safety review of nuclear cargo. Critics dismissed the subsequent report as merely a list of the year's nuclear waste events. The Blair government did not propose adopting a single recommendation.

Greenpeace asked the nuclear consultant, John Large, to examine the whole scenario of transporting nuclear waste on trains. The waste is stored in 30cm-thick forged steel flasks which have been rigorously fire-tested and drop-tested. Even so, John Large points out that these flasks would not withstand a typical train-tunnel fire where the temperature can reach one thousand degrees Celsius. In such an eventuality, water would be forced out of the flasks and the fuel inside would ignite. The subsequent radiation could be spread over six kilometres and could kill and maim many people, resulting in a legacy of cancers and other diseases. In 2011, thousands of tonnes of nuclear waste were being moved across many countries and through densely populated cities. The pro-nuclear lobby believes that an accident cannot happen under any circumstances. This is a rather naïve and dangerous position to take in a world where suicide bombers set out to cause maximum damage and loss of life.[25]

A plan to transport forty four tonnes of radioactive uranium and plutonium by rail has been opposed by British County Councils which are concerned about the possibility of accidents or terrorists attacks. In late August 2011, it emerged that the Nuclear Decommissioning Authority (NDA) plans to make about fifty rail shipments from the Dounreay nuclear power station at Caithness, Scotland to Sellafield in Cumbria.[26] This is a journey

25. Madeleine Brettingham, 'Tracking hazard,' *The Guardian*, Society/Guardian /Environment, 31 May 2006, p. 8.
26. Rob Edwards, 'Councils oppose new nuclear train plan,' *The Guardian*, 27 August 2011, p. 2.

of five hundred kilometres. A group called Nuclear-Free Local Authorities claims that the plan breaches important environmental principles – one of which is that radioactive waste should be managed as close as possible to where it is produced. They also point out that there is a risk that terrorists might hijack the trains and steal nuclear material which might be used to make dirty bombs or crude nuclear weapons. In response to this argument, the NDA point out that the nuclear material from Dounreay is not nuclear waste but nuclear material from a fast-breeder reactor programme that requires appropriate management. They also remind those opposed to transporting nuclear waste that nuclear material has been transported on a daily basis across Britain for over half a century without any incidents to date. George Regan, the chair of the Nuclear-Free Local Authorities and a Labour councilor in Dundee, is not convinced. 'I am very worried about the movement of such sensitive material across Scotland to Sellafield.'[27]

The fact that some nuclear waste can remain hazardous for hundreds of thousands of years makes people very nervous about creating long-term repositories of nuclear waste in their communities. Apart from the difficulty of finding a site which is suitable from a geological and hydrological perspective, people have great difficulty dealing with such long-term projects. After all, modern humans left Africa only about 80,000 years ago. 250,000 years ago, our ancestors did not have the full range of verbal skills. Human beings only developed full speech patterns about 120,000 years ago. Given this history is it reasonable to think that human beings will be able to store plutonium safely for 200,000 years?

27. Ibid.

CHAPTER EIGHT

Nuclear Power or Renewable Energy

Permission given in 2003 to build the Olkiluoto nuclear reactor in Finland was seen as a great boost for the nuclear industry, not just in Europe, but right around the world. In 2004, the contract price for building a 1,600 megawatt nuclear power station was €3.2 billion. Olkiluoto is 315 kilometres north-west of Helsinki in Finland. Work on the reactor began in August 2005. By August 2009, energy consultant Steve Thomas believed that the scale of the problems encountered while building the Olkiluoto nuclear power station means that the cost would be in the region of €5.7 billion.[1]

Proponents claim that its walls are thick enough to withstand a plane crashing into the plant. They claim that it also has many more safety features than earlier reactors and could withstand a storm-surge of up to eleven feet. The tsunami on the north-east coast of Japan was much higher than this.[2]

Olkiluoto has been plagued with faulty material and planning problems since work began in 2005. It is now four years behind schedule and is expected to begin generating electricity in 2013. It has also run very much over budget. The final estimate is still €5.7 billion, which means that it will cost close to €3,500 per kilowatt.[3]

If it takes almost ten years to obtain planning permission and to build a nuclear plant, this form of energy can hardly be a serious contender for providing power in the future. The lead time for new plants has often to include upgrading the grid with high-voltage power lines, which also must be cleared for safety considerations by the planning authorities.[4]

Proponents of nuclear energy forget that the industry has benefited from massive government subsidies. In the US, for example, during the past fifteen years, the amount of energy produced by wind and nuclear power was almost similar.

1. Paul Dorfman, 'Who to trust on nuclear?' *The Guardian*, 14 April 2011, p. 27.
2. Matti Huuhtanen, 'Disaster Proofing,' *The Irish Examiner*, 29 March 2011, p. 13.
3. http://www.worldwatch.org/nuclear-power-after-fukushima p. 5.
4. Ibid., p. 12.

Nuclear energy produced 2.6 billion kWh, while wind energy produced 1.9 billion kWh. The taxpayers' subsidy to the nuclear industry was forty times more than that given to wind energy – $900 million as against $39.4 million.[5] It seems clear, even before the Fukushima crisis occurred, that 'the economics of nuclear power are such that government subsidies are almost always required to support private sector construction of nuclear plants. Yet, in many countries that wish to develop nuclear energy, limited government resources compete with pressing needs from health, education and poverty-reduction programmes.'[6]

Peak Uranium

One of the reasons often given for building nuclear power plants is that oil resources are running out and, therefore, nuclear plants are needed to provide energy for our modern world. However, what people forget is that uranium is not very abundant in the world. In fact, it is a rare metal and is often found in parts of the world that are politically unstable. The nuclear industry is even under pressure now as it tries to meet the uranium needs of the current number of reactors. In 2010, for example, the 440 or more nuclear power plants in the world consumed 68,000 tonnes of uranium. Out of that total, 55,000 tonnes came from the mining industry and the rest from reprocessed fuel, recycled atomic warheads and other military sources. When these recycling programmes come to an end, sourcing uranium will become a real problem for the industry.[7] Due to multiple uncertainties, there is little investment in opening new uranium mines. According to Jean Nortier, chief executive of Uranium One, a mining and exploration company based in Vancouver, Canada, 'current prices are much too low to provide the incentive needed to meet the medium and long-term demand for uranium.'[8] (The price of

5. Antony Froggart and Mycle Schneider, *Systems for Change: Nuclear Power Vs Energy Efficiency and Renewables*, Heinrich Boll Stiftung Publication on Ecology, February 2010, p. 46.

6. http://www.worldwatch.org/nuclear-power-after-fukushima, p. 17.

7. Andrew McKillop, 'Peak Uranium and other Threats to Nuclear Power,' 14 April 2011. http://www.marketoracle.co.uk/Article 27549.html.

8. Justin Mullins, 'Warning on global uranium supplies,' *NewScientist*, 28 November 2009, p. 10.

uranium had fallen from a peak of $130 per pound of uranium oxide in 2007 to $45 per pound in 2009).

Many scientists are also questioning the estimates which the Nuclear Energy Agency (NEA) cited in what has been called The Red Book. The 2007 Red Book estimated that there were 5.5 million tonnes of uranium that can be mined for less than $130 per kilo. The 2008 Red Book had the estimate at 4.7 million tonnes. Michael Dittmar, a particle physicist at CERN in Geneva, has criticised these estimates. He points out that in Niger, the estimates of the amount of uranium available has fluctuated widely in the past decade. He is on record as saying that the geology of the region does not support such fluctuations. Other factors such as political maneuvering come into play. Robert Vance, a nuclear scientist who works as an analyst at NEA, says that, while he cannot rule out such factors, there are strict rules governing resource estimation. 'We work hard to ensure that the data is reliable.'[9] He also points to the fact that it is possible to increase the mining of uranium in some countries. Kazakhstan, for example, has increased the production of uranium by thirty per cent per annum. Mining companies face much stricter regulations in developed countries. Given this uncertain scenario, Dittmar is convinced that 'Western countries planning to expand their nuclear capacity without their source of uranium ought to be looking at the figures very closely.'[10]

Given the dangers of nuclear power and the massive cost overruns in building nuclear power stations, governments must abandon their policy of pretending that nuclear and renewable energy can thrive together. Governments should focus on promoting research and development into a range of possible renewable energy technologies and, also, on promoting energy efficiency. This will not be easy as large oil companies have huge influence with governments. But unless there is massive investment in a range of renewable energy sources, the future scenario for energy will be quite bleak. People such as Jeremy Leggett, geologist and writer on the energy crisis and climate

9. Ibid.
10. Ibid.

change, argue that by 2013, solar energy will be as cheap as energy from conventional sources.[11] The big difference, in terms of energy policy is that fossil fuel energy is finite and causes global warming, whereas solar energy will not run out for a few billion years, at least.

Nuclear Power is Not Very 'Green'

The champions of nuclear power now use the connection between burning fossil fuel and global warming as a way of rehabilitating the nuclear power industry. This is the reason given by John Hutton for the UK Labour government's U-turn on nuclear power. If one looks merely at the generation of electricity in the nuclear plant itself, then it is true that very little fossil fuel is used. But the nuclear cycle from beginning to end is a much more extensive operation than what happens in the nuclear plant. An enormous quantity of fossil fuel is needed at almost every phase of the nuclear process – a process which begins with uranium mining.

However, far from solving our problems with carbon, nuclear reactors may well be vulnerable to the consequences of climate change. Nuclear power stations need large volumes of water to cool the reactors. This is why many of them are built near the sea or large river estuaries. However, waters are subject to major storm surges and a rise in sea-levels, as a result of melting icecaps and expanding seas, caused by climate change. But that is not all. According to Natalie Kopytko from the environment department at the University of York in Britain, these waters can be disrupted by water scarcity and a rise in the water temperature.[12] She believes that hurricanes pose the greatest threat to nuclear power plants, because most climate scientists predict a dramatic increase in hurricane intensity as temperatures rise across the globe. Flooding is also a major worry, as was seen at Fukushima, but droughts can be equally devastating. Heat waves, due to climate change, also pose problems. The lower the temperature of the cooling water entering the reactor, the more electricity can be

11. http://www.jeremyleggett.net/solar-revolution.
12. Natalie Kopytko, 'Nuclear summer?,' *NewScientist*, 21 May 2011, p. 22.

generated. During the heatwave in France in 2003, surface water became so warm that many nuclear reactors had to be shut down.

UN Study States that Renewable Energy Technologies Could Meet the World's Energy Needs
In the first week of May 2011, a thousand-word report from the Intergovernmental Panel on Climate Change (IPCC), examined how renewable energy technologies could meet the energy needs of the world. The report was entitled Renewable Energy Sources and Climate Change Mitigation (SRREN). It claims that almost eighty per cent of the world's energy supply could come from renewable sources, especially solar, within forty years. The report added the *caveat* that this goal could only be achieved if governments pursue the policies needed to promote green power.[13]

The IPCC Report also claims that 'if the full range of renewable technologies were deployed, the world could keep greenhouse gas concentrations to less than 450 parts per million, the level scientists have predicted will be the limit of safety beyond which climate change becomes catastrophic and irreversible.'[14]

The chairman of the IPCC, Rajendra Pachauri, argues that it would cost the world one per cent of GDP to achieve this desirable goal. The Report acknowledges that renewable energy contribution to global energy output has increased rapidly in recent years. Of the 300 gigawatts of new electricity generation capacity added globally between 2008 and 2009, about 140 gigawatts came from renewable sources, such as wind and solar power.

To achieve the goals set out in the report, it will be necessary to invest $5 trillion in the next decade, with an increase to $7 trillion from 2021 to 2030. Ramon Pichs, who was the co-chair of the IPCC working group said, 'The report shows that it is not the availability of [renewable] resources but the public policies that will either expand or constrain renewable energy development over the coming decades. Developing countries have an important stake

13. Fiona Harvey, 'Renewable Energy Can Power the World, Says Landmark UN Study,' *The Guardian*, 9 May 2011. http://www.guardian.co.uk/environment/2011/may/09/ipcc-renewable-energy-power-world. Print downloaded on 9 May 2011.
14. Ibid.

in the future – as these countries are where most of the seven billion people of the world live. Many of these people do not currently have access to electricity, despite the fact that favourable conditions for developing renewable energy exist in these places.'[15]

In 2008, about thirteen percent of the world's energy came from renewable sources. Wind power was responsible for two percent of global energy. Unfortunately, about ten percent of the world's energy requirements came from burning biomass. This is not sustainable, as it leads to deforestation, soil erosion, an increase in CO_2 emissions and respiratory problems for those who burn carbon to cook their food.

Renewable Energy

Solar energy, using photovoltaic (PV) technology is a benign source of energy. It is generated when sunlight hits the pure crystals of a semiconductor material such as silicon. In the process, the electrons are prised loose from the atoms to which they are attached and produce an electric current. It is not a new technology. The first PV cell was created by Bell Labs in the United States in 1954. The efficiency rate of the first cell was only six per cent. That efficiency rate has grown dramatically in the past decade. According to Allen Barnett at the University of Delaware, efficiency rates have now reached over forty per cent and this can be further improved with more research and development. Furthermore, with new investment, production costs are falling which means that the cost of solar generated electricity is coming closer to the price of fossil fuel generated electricity.

One would think that the photovoltaic capital of the world would be the sunny Mediterranean or Australia. However, this is not the case. Germany claims that it has half of the world's installed capacity for photovoltaic. The key to Germany's success was neither geography nor its technological prowess, but its political will. In 2003, the German government introduced the first large scale 'feed-in' tariff system. This means that every producer of solar-generated energy, whether they are home

15. Ibid.

owners or producing it on a vast, commercial scale, can sell their
excess power back to the grid and receive a premium price which
is, in fact, three times that received by conventional producers of
electricity. Within two years, almost 300,000 individuals and small
businesses had installed photovoltaic systems on their rooftops.
By 2007, the country had three gigawatts of solar power which is
the equivalent of three large scale, fossil fuel generating stations. In
the past two years, twenty countries, including Italy and Spain and
some states in the US, such as California, have followed the
German lead.

On the cost side, the authors of the IPCC Special Report on
Renewable Energy Sources and Climate Change Mitigation
(SRREN), pointed out that solar energy is still more expensive
than fossil fuel energy.[16] It will mean that production will have to
increase, across the spectrum of renewable energies by a factor of
twenty, if we are to avoid the worst aspects of climate change.

One of the authors of the Report, Sven Teske, from
Greenpeace, said that the Report is an invitation to governments
to initiate a radical overhaul of their policies and to place renewable
energy at the centre of their energy policies. The report is a
disappointment to those people who are promoting wave and
tidal energy. It found that these 'were unlikely to significantly
contribute to the global energy supply before 2020'.[17] The
European Commission, however, has appointed leading Irish
ocean energy researchers to coordinate a €9 million test programme, aimed at accelerating the development of ocean
renewable energy technologies. The programme will be run at
University College Cork's Hydraulic and Maritime Research
Centre. For a number of years, this centre has played a leading
role in researching wave potential. Within the EU, Ireland and
Scotland have the most active Atlantic wave systems. According
to a joint Republic and Northern Ireland Report on wave energy

16. IPCC Special Report on Renewable Energy Sources and Climate Change
Mitigation (SRREN).
Why is the IPCC working on a Special Report on Renewable Energy Sources and
Climate Change Mitigation. http://www.ipcc.ch/pdf/press/ipcc_leaflets_
2010/ipcc_srren_leaflet.pdf.
17. Ibid.

published early in 2011, a 'fully developed' all-Ireland ocean energy sector could be worth about €9 billion by 2030.[18]

A report from the Consultancy firm, Ernst and Young, in June 2011, predicted that the price of solar panels is falling so fast that, by 2013, they will cost only half of the price that was paid for solar panels as recently as 2009.[19] Such a study involves comparing the relative cost of solar energy with other forms of energy. The crucial question is: how does the economics of solar power compare, in terms of the dollar price of each watt of power at peak capacity, with other forms of energy?

In this study, Ernst and Young base their prediction on the fact that the average one-off installation costs for solar photovoltaic (PV) panels has, in fact, already dropped considerably in relation to the 2009 price. They are convinced that this reduction will continue. At present, PV installations in Britain are competitive because they are subsidised by the taxpayer. The study, which is based on the analysis of brokers and industry analysis, predicts that large scale solar installations will be cost effective in 2013 without government subsidies. As the cost of PV solar panels plummet, the cost of fossil fuel energy will continue to rise. The chair of the Solar Trade Association (STA) Howard Johns, said the current subsidy for PV makes good economic sense because it contributes to building the capacity of the industry and this will further drive costs down. The medium-term result of these progressive policies is that unsubsidised solar energy will become much more widespread and available.[20] The conclusion which the Ernst and Young study reached contrasts with the views of the British government's Committee on Climate Change (CCC). They have argued that solar power is still too expensive to warrant serious consideration at the present time. Ben Warren, who conducted the study for Ernst and Young, argues that the CCC perspective does not take into account the wider economic benefits of solar energy. He told *The Guardian* that, 'being a laggard

18. Lorna Siggins, 'UCC to run €9m wave energy trials,' *The Irish Times*, 1 December 2011, p. 2.
19. Duncan Clark, 'Solar energy will soon make commercial sense as panel costs plummet,' says Ernst & Young, *The Guardian*, 21 June 2011, p. 25.
20. Ibid.

has never been very successful in terms of capturing the greater share of the value added for the economy ... If you create a sustainable market, you will achieve cost savings and drive economic benefits in terms of tax income and job creation.'[21]

The Ernst and Young study predicts that by 2016-19, companies which use a lot of electricity will find it cheaper to buy non-subsidised solar energy than to buy their electricity directly from the national grid. The Climate Minister, Greg Barker, seems to agree with Ernst and Young's view. He told *The Guardian* that 'Britain had underestimated the potential of solar energy and, in the light of falling prices, he hopes to find "new pathways" for supporting large-scale solar developments.'[22] Market analysts, Bloomberg New Energy Finance (BNEF), point out the price of solar panels fell by almost fifty per cent in 2011. Solar energy now costs one quarter of what it did in 2008 which will make it a cost-effective option for many people in northern and especially southern countries. In 2011, solar panels generated twenty-seven gigawatts compared with only 7.7 GW in 2008.[23]

Finally, Ben Warren makes a very important point when he draws attention to the fact that 'the energy market is starved of capital – it won't come from utilities and banks. There's a desperate need to engage with institutional investors.'[24] Governments, too, should be investing in solar energy in order to de-carbonise their economies and thus avoid catastrophic climate change. However, if billions are invested in new nuclear reactors, then there will be less money left to invest in solar and wind energy.

The rise in oil prices in recent years and the need to curb greenhouse gas emissions has given a new impetus to solar energy. One reason why photovoltaic has not developed elsewhere is because it is still more expensive than fossil fuel. The rapid growth in the technology and the escalating cost of fossil fuel will reduce the cost significantly. Energy economists estimate that the cost falls by roughly one fifth every time the capacity doubles.

21. Ibid.
22. Ibid.
23. Michal Marshall, 'Panel price crash could spark solar revolution,' *NewScientist*, 4 February 2012, p. 12.
24. Ibid.

There is intense interest in researching the viability of a range of other photovoltaic materials, apart from silicon. In December 2007, a start-up company in California printed solar cells on aluminium film. These cells are extremely light and flexible. The company claims that it will be able to produce electricity for ninety-nine US cents per watt. This would bring the cost in line with electricity generated from coal.

Solar Power on the Rise

As a missionary, I am aware that photovoltaic technology has great potential in poorer countries. In the early 1980s, we kept vaccines in a solar-power fridge in Mindanao in the Philippines. Greenpeace and the European PV Industry Association published a report in 2001 entitled, 'Solar Generation: Solar Electricity for over 1 Billion People and 2 Million Jobs by 2020'. The document envisages two hundred gigawatts of installed PV capacity worldwide supplying one billion off-grid and eighty-two million grid-connected users. Over thirty million of these would be in Europe. By 2020, some sixty per cent of PV production would be located in Asia, Africa and Latin America.

In 2012, in places such as India, electricity from solar panels is cheaper than energy from diesel generators. This is why India plans to install 20,000 megawatts of solar power by 2022. Electricity from solar panels supplied to the grid has fallen from just 8.78 rupees per kilowatt-hour, compared with 17 rupees for diesel. Bjorn Emde, the European spokesman for Suntech, the world's largest producer of silicon panels, says that 'we have been selling to Asia and Middle East.'[25]

The charity, Christian Aid, believes that smallscale solar power is the best option for millions of small communities who, at present, lack electricity. Photovoltaic technology would enable poor countries to generate electricity economically without building massive electrical grids. This energy revolution could be similar to the one which mobile phone technology promoted in the area of communication during the past twenty years.

25. Ibid.

Ordinary people in poor countries can now communicate with each other, without the country having to install, expensive, land based telecommunication systems. Churches could support this technology by investing in research and installing PV technology. Installing solar panels is still more expensive than buying a diesel engine but Suntech also predicts that, by 2015, solar electric will be as cheap as electricity from the grid in half of the countries of the world.[26]

In Article 29 of the encyclical *Caritas in Veritate*, Pope Benedict XVI links the need to protect the environment with consideration about energy needs in both rich and poor countries:

> On this front too, there is a pressing moral need for renewed solidarity, especially in relationships between developing countries and those that are highly industrialised. The technologically advanced societies can and must lower their domestic energy consumption, either through an evolution in manufacturing methods or through greater ecological sensitivity among their citizens. It should be added that at present it is possible to achieve improved energy efficiency while at the same time encouraging research into alternative forms of energy. What is needed, though, is a worldwide redistribution of energy resources, so that countries lacking those resources can have access to them.[27]

The Pope returned to this theme in his World Day of Peace Message entitled, *If You Want to Cultivate Peace, Protect Creation*, on 1 January 2010:

> To be sure, among the basic problems which the international community has to address is that of energy resources and the development of joint and sustainable strategies to satisfy the energy needs of present and future generations. This means that technologically advanced societies must be prepared to encourage more sober

26. Ibid.
27. Pope Benedict XVI, *Caritas in Veritate*, Libreria Editrice Vaticana, Vatican City, July 2009, par. 49.

lifestyles, while reducing their energy consumption and improving its efficiency. At the same time there is a need to encourage research into, and utilisation of, forms of energy with lower impact on the environment and a worldwide redistribution of energy resources, so that countries lacking those resources can have access to them.'[28]

Smart-Grid Technology
There are other innovations on the horizon which will improve energy efficiency dramatically. Smart-grid technology will make it possible for consumers to control the energy they are using at any one time. James Wilson who lives in Fayetteville, North Carolina, is part of a pilot project which is being run jointly by Fayetteville Public Works Commission, IBM and Consert, a smart-grid company based in Raleigh, North Carolina. By using the internet and his mobile phone to control when appliances are turned on and off in his home, he has managed to reduce his consumption of electricity by forty per cent.[29]

Smart-grid technology will also help utility companies. The current way of delivering electricity has hardly changed in a century. It involves having large power plants to generate huge quantities of electricity which is then transmitted over long distances. In the process, large amounts of power are lost. In order to get electricity, every customer has to connect to this large grid. A meter on the premises calculates how much electricity is used and a bill is sent to the customer at the end of each month.

Smart-grid technology aims to give both the utility company and the consumer near-real time knowledge about how much energy is being used. The bedrock of this technology is the smart-meter which gives accurate information to the customer and supplier about how much energy is being used at any one time. Until the advent of the smart-grid, the way utility companies met their peak load demands was by building more power plants or buying in power from other utilities. Smart-grid technology will allow the utilities to manage their output in a more effective way.

28. Pope Benedict XVI, 'If you want to cultivate peace, protect creation,' par. 9.
29. Kurt Kleiner, 'Knowledge is Power,' *NewScientist*, 13 November 2010, p. i.

For example, since 2003, the city of Austin in Texas has been at the forefront of this technology and 90,000 consumers have agreed to let the utility turn off their air conditioners for ten minutes every half hour during peak demand. The company sends a radio signal to the smart thermostats to shut down for ten minutes. This reduces peak demand by forty megawatts for these periods.[30] The smart-grid technology allows customers to make major saving by using appliances, such as dishwashers, when the price is low during off-peak hours. The smart-grid will also benefit consumers who use photo voltaic or other technologies to generate electricity themselves.

It makes sense for governments to invest heavily in this marriage between power generation and information technology. In 2009, the US government announced a $3.4 billion award for smart-meter projects and a further $620 to support pilot projects in various parts of the country. Smart-grid technology is still only in its infancy, but, even now, it is clear that it is introducing a revolution in the way electricity is generated and consumed.

---

30. Ibid., p iii.

CHAPTER NINE

The Catholic Church and Nuclear Power

I am sure that there is no chapter on prayer in any manual describing how to deal with a nuclear emergency in a nuclear power plant. Mixing prayer with nuclear physics and technology is so alien to modern science that the very thought of it might draw peals of laughter. Yet, prayer ran like a thread through an hour-long programme entitled *Japan – Inside the Meltdown* which was screened on BBC Two on 23 February 2012 at 9.00 p.m. The programme gave an hour by hour description of the crucial moment when a severe earthquake and subsequent tsunami swamped the reactors at the Fukushima Daiichi nuclear power plant. Key witnesses, including the Prime Minister, Naota Kan, the Director of the Fukushima Daiichi nuclear plant, Mr Masao Yoshida, senior management at Tepco, workers at the nuclear plant, army personnel and firefighters gave graphic accounts of what happened and how close things came to a complete nuclear meltdown which could have made huge areas of Japan uninhabitable for decades.

One of the most extraordinary things about the programme was that everyone, from the prime minister down, seemed to be praying that a catastrophe would be avoided. One worker, who was about to enter the plant to manually open the vents, described a conversation he had with his wife. He realised he was risking his own life by entering into the stricken nuclear plant and exposing himself to deadly levels of radiation. Given these risks, his wife was obviously very worried but, as the conversation ended, she said she would be praying for him.

Mixing religion and spirituality with nuclear science and technology, while not covered in the official handbooks, is not so alien to those who are at the coal-face, particularly when accidents occur. There are just over half a million Catholics in Japan or just over 0.5 per cent of the total population. Nevertheless, soon after the Fukushima disaster, the Japanese bishops issued a statement stating their continued concern about the Fukushima nuclear accident that followed the 11 March 2011 earthquake and tsunami. A Japanese bishop told the Fides news agency that he opposed the construction of nuclear power plants worldwide. The Auxiliary Bishop of Osaka, Michael Goro Matsuura said:

> Together with the Justice and Peace Commission of the Japanese Bishops, which I headed up until last year, we have raised awareness to fight the construction of new nuclear power plants in Japan and globally. I believe that this serious incident should be a lesson for Japan and for the entire planet, and will be an incentive to abandon these projects. We call on the solidarity of Christians worldwide to support this campaign.[1]

Canada

In June 2009, the Catholic Bishops of Alberta in Canada issued a document entitled *Pastoral Reflections on Nuclear Energy in Alberta*. The bishops pointed to the 'serious ethical questions that must be adequately addressed before a decision (on nuclear power) is reached and implemented'.[2] They questioned whether there was sufficient river water available to meet the needs of the proposed nuclear power plant in Alberta. They argued that there are other ways of reducing greenhouse gases. In the face of the potential risks to human beings and the environment, the bishops called attention to the 'precautionary principle'. This moral principle states that, if an action can potentially cause major harm to human beings or the environment, in the absence of a scientific consensus that the action will not be harmful, the burden of proof that it will not be harmful lies with those who are proposing the action, not with those who are opposing it. The bishops, like many others, are aware that nuclear power plants or trains carrying nuclear waste are vulnerable to terrorist attacks. They discussed the cost and value for money of going down the nuclear route and highlighted the fact there has been a cost overrun in building many nuclear

---

1. http://www.fides.org/aree/news/newsdet.php?idnews=28687&lan=eng. Downloaded on 6 April 2011.
2. http://www.caedm.ca/book/export/html/145. Downloaded on 5 April 2011.

reactors.[3] The pastoral letter called attention to the lack of a permanent place to store nuclear waste. This means that future generations will have to deal with this carcinogenic and toxic legacy. They also point out that the risk posed by nuclear reactors is such that it is impossible to get full insurance cover for a nuclear reactor.

Germany

Four days before the German government agreed to phase out all Germany's nuclear reactors by 2022, the German Bishops' conference published a fifty-two page document in which it repeated its call to the government to shut down their nuclear reactors as soon as possible. They stated that the production of nuclear energy was 'unethical'. The document, which was published on 26 May 2011, was prepared by a commission of experts under the leadership of Cardinal Reinhard Marx of Munich. The cardinal was also a member of the German Government's Ethics Commission on Safe Energy which recently published a report calling for an end to the use of nuclear power.[4] Writing in *Frankfurter Allgemeine Zeitung* on 29 May 2011, Cardinal Reinhard Marx said that he felt a technology that had incalculable consequences for entire generations could not be trusted.[5]

Korea

In an article in the monthly magazine *Kyeonghyan*, the president of the Korean Bishops' Conference, Bishop Peter Kang U-il of Cheju, wrote that nuclear power is a monster which cannot co-exist with living things. He stated that it is a lie to say that nuclear power is a green or clean energy. He urged the Korean government to review its energy policy. He said that a visit to Japan in October 2011 to deliver aid to the tsunami-hit Saitama and Sendai dioceses, made him question whether nuclear power is really

---

3. Ibid.
4. Christa Pongratz-Lippitt, 'Bishops applaud nuclear phase-out,' *The Tablet*, 4 June 2011, p. 30.
5. http://nuclear-news.net/2011/04/04/germn-public-churches-oppose-nuclear-energy-prefer-more-modest-lifestyle.

safe.[6] Bishop Peter Kang speaks Japanese fluently which meant he could talk directly to people affected by the disaster at the Fukushima Daiichi nuclear power plant. He went on to say that everyone needs to pay attention to nuclear power as it could lead to a catastrophe. Citing Pope Benedict's encyclical, *Caritas in Veritate*, he said: 'Our natural environment is God's gift to everyone, and we must take care of it as we have a responsibility towards the poor, future generations and humanity as a whole.' Bishop Kang said that the God-given right to rule the earth is not absolute. 'We must limit ourselves when it comes to nature,' he said, adding that 'nuclear power is beyond that limit.'

Nuclear power, he asserted, is a potential 'great disaster which can't be controlled by any human technology'. He, therefore, urged people to reflect on society's preoccupation with consumerism, which has led to its consuming too much energy.

On 14 December 2011, Tetsuji Imanaka, assistant professor at the Research Reactor Institute of Kyoto University in Japan, addressed some one hundred priests, nuns and lay people. Bishop Matthias Ri Iong-hoon, president of the Korean Bishops' Committee for Justice and Peace also attended. The bishops said that there is no safe nuclear power, despite a government assurance of safe nuclear energy. Imanaka added that the Japanese government has stressed that 'nuclear power plants are safe whatever may happen'. Yet, the authorities already knew that a nuclear plant disaster would cause a massive amount of damage. He was convinced that the Japanese government was not telling the truth about nuclear power.[7] Bishop Ri Iong-hoon asked the participants to protest against the government's stubborn attitude in pushing ahead with its nuclear plan while covering up the danger of nuclear power. South Korea has twenty-one nuclear reactors and is building or planning to build eleven more, according to the Korea Hydro and Nuclear Power Company.

---

6. Nuclear power 'monster', Bishop warns. Posted by Ivan on 18 May 2011 at 4:58 p.m., UCAN News. www.ucanews.com/2011/05/18/check-nuclear-power-a-monster-bishop-warns/print.

7. Posted by johnb, 'Nuclear power not safe, says expert,' UCAN news, 15 December 2011, http://www.ucanews.com/2011/12/15/nuclear-power-not-safe-says-expert/print.

On 4 January 2012, an anti-nuclear association accused local government of failing to implement safety measures after a recent radiation leak at a power plant in Busan, South Korea. At a news conference, the anti-Nuclear Association said that the leak would not have occurred if stringent regulations and inspections had been implemented.[8]

Jeong Su-hee, the Association's spokesperson, said the leak was an accident waiting to happen. According to her, 'The factory responsible for the leak was warned about possible dangers from the Institute of Nuclear Safety during an inspection last March. But they did not correct any defects and the inspection was not followed up.'[9] The Association called for medical checks for the 30,000 people working in the area. Father Vincentius Kim Jun-han, president of Busan Diocesan's Committee for Justice and Peace, said, 'We will keep monitoring radiation levels in suspected contaminated areas.'[10] He said that his committee will continue various campaigns against the use of nuclear power.

On 23 December 2011, the Korea Hydro and Nuclear Power (KHNP) announced that it had selected two sites – one in Samcheok city and the other in Yeongdeok-gun county on the east coast – as the location for two nuclear power plants. Three days later, on 26 December 2011, in response to this announcement, the leadership of the Catholic Church in Korea renewed its demand that the government stop building nuclear power plants.[11] The No Nukes Samcheok Coalition said a growing number of people were opposed to the plan and people's opinions were not reflected in the selection process. Father Paul Park Hong-pyo, a coalition spokesman, said: 'The disaster at the Fukushima nuclear power plant in Japan in March 2011 has turned people against nuclear power.'[12] After the Fukushima incident, just over half the population was against the plan and

8. 'Anger over radioactive leak,' UCAN news, 4 January 2012, http://www.ucanews. com/2012/01/04/anger-over-radioactive-leak/print.
9. Ibid.
10. Ibid.
11. Church voices anger at nuclear plan, http://www.ucanews.com/2011/12/27 /church-voices-anger-at-nuclear-plan.
12. Ibid.

that number had increased significantly since then. 'I think three quarters of them are against the idea,' he said.[13]

The Wonju diocesan Committee for Justice and Peace called on the government to reject the application. The diocese, which includes Samcheok, called the KHNP decision a 'unilateral' action because what was happening was the 'violence by the state against the people.'[14] The committee also said the government's aim to increase the number of nuclear power plants goes against growing global opposition to nuclear energy.

In January 2012, a number of dioceses in South Korea announced the setting up of a new anti-nuclear group supported by the bishops. The new group, the East Coast Solidarity for Anti-Nuke, was formed by the Justice and Peace committees of the four dioceses of Andong, Busan, Daegu and Wonju.[15]

India

In November 2011, rumours circulated that Bishop Yvon Ambroise of Tuticorin diocese had distanced himself from the people's protest against the Kudankulam Nuclear Power Project (KNPP) in Tamil Nadu. On 9 November 2011, the bishop issued a statement saying that he was 'morally and spiritually' with his people.[16] He went on to say that, 'As per the Catholic Church's teachings and the Tamil Nadu Bishop Council's resolution, I continue to show my solidarity with my people who are under great fear and anxiety concerning the Kudankulam Nuclear Plant.'[17]

The bishop has been nominated to be a member of the state-level panel which was set up to interact with a fifteen member Central group of experts from the Department of Atomic Energy (DAE) in India. The bishop did not attend the first meeting which

---

13. Ibid.
14. Ibid.
15. 'Dioceses set up anti-nuclear group,' ucanews.com staff, Seoul, Korea, 16 January 2012. http://www.ucanews.com/2012/01/16/dioceses-set-up-anti-nuclear-group.
16. George Anthony, 'Tuticorin Bishop clarifies stand on Kudankulam nuclear plant row,' *Christian India Today*, 10 November 2010. http://in.christiantoday.com/articles/tuticorin-bishop-clarifies-stand-on-kudankulam-nuclear-plant-row/6810.html.
17. Ibid.

took place at Tirunelvi because he said that he had no expertise in the area of assessing the risks posed by nuclear reactors which used Russian technology. He felt that someone from the KNPP protest group would be better able to represent those who were opposed to the opening of the nuclear power plant. On 22 September 2011, the Tamil Nadu government passed a resolution urging India's prime minister, Manmohan Singh, and the central government, to halt work at Kudankulam till the fears of the people were allayed.

On 15 November 2011, police charged Bishop Yvon Ambroise, and four parish priests with aiding and supporting a protest against the Koodankulam nuclear power plant in the southern state of Tamil Nadu. The bishop, priests and some social activists were also charged with illegal assembly and preventing government officials from carrying out official work at the construction site in Koodankulam. The bishop believes that the case is a tactic designed to create fear among the protestors. But he added, 'We are undeterred by the charges filed by the local police and the struggle will go on.'[18]

Bishop Ambroise said, 'We were objecting to the plant from the beginning but after the Fukushima disaster in Japan, people have also understood the problems with nuclear energy and are protesting against the plant.'[19] He clarified that the anti-nuclear agitation was a people's movement and not a church-led movement. The prelate said he also suspected that police action was taken because of Hindu right-wing groups who are against the protest.

The Republic of the Philippines

In February 2009, the Catholic Bishops' Conference of the Philippines (CBCP) issued a statement opposing the rehabilitation of the Bataan Nuclear Power Plant (BNPP). The Plant was completed but never fueled. It is situated on the Bataan Peninsula, Morong, which is one hundred kilometres west of Manila.

---

18. Posted by johnb, UCAN News, 16 November, 2011. http://www.ucanews.com /2011/11/16/police-charge-protest-bishop/print. Downloaded on 29 February 2012.
19. Ibid.

In a pastoral statement, the CBCP urged the Philippine Congress to 'completely and irrevocably reject the opening of the nuclear plant as the most dangerous and expensive way to generate electricity'.[20] The statement was issued by the then CBCP president, Archbishop Angelo Lagdameo, of the Archdiocese of Jaro, Iloilo City on the Island of Panay. He went on to state that the multiple risks and possibilities of corruption outweigh the supposed benefits. They recommended that the facility at Morong, in the province of Bataan, Philippines, be mothballed.

On 17 March 2011, the Catholic bishops of the Philippines issued a statement claiming that the crisis at the Japanese nuclear power plant vindicated their opposition to the development of peaceful nuclear power. Bishop Deogracias Iñiquez, who is the chairperson of the Filipino Bishops' Public-Affairs Committee, said that 'what is happening in Japan right now confirmed our fears'. The bishops' conference has consistently opposed building nuclear power plants.[21] There are no nuclear power plants active in the Philippines today. The current president of the Philippines, Benigno Aquino III, is on record as saying that the mothballed Bataan nuclear reactor will never be used for its original purpose.

The Philippines government is bound by a twenty-five year moratorium on the use of nuclear energy which expires in 2022. The government says it remains open to harnessing nuclear energy as a long-term solution to growing electricity demand, and since the Fukushima accident, its Department of Science and Technology (DOST) has been making public pronouncements in favour of pursuing nuclear energy.

The nuclear power plant, which never generated a watt of electricity, is now a tourist attraction both for Filipinos and overseas visitors. Reynaldo Punzalan, a technician who has been

---

20. Dona Pazzibugan, Alcuin Papa Christian V. Esguerra and Leila B. Salaverria, 'Recommends Bataan facility "must be dismantled",' *Philippine Daily Enquirer*, 27 February 2009.
21. http://www.catholicculture.org/news/headlines/index.cfm?storyid=9645&utm_source=feedburner&utm_medium=feed&utm_campaign=Feed%3A+CatholicWorldNewsFeatureStories+%28Catholic+World+News+%28on+Catholic Culture.org%29%29

working at the plant since 1979, tells the tourists that 'It's only here in the world what you can enter a reactor containment building and see for yourself a real reactor.'[22]

Given the opposition of the Catholic Church and many Civil Society Organisations in the Philippines, the DOST officials acknowledge that the Fukushima accident has set back their job of winning the public over to nuclear energy by four or five years. This has not stopped the Philippine government from attempting to build capacity in various aspects of nuclear science and technology. The country, however, lacks the technical expertise to operate a nuclear power station safely. Carmencita Bariso, assistant director of the Department of Energy's planning bureau, says that, despite the Fukushima accident, her organisation has continued with a study on the viability, safety and social acceptability of nuclear energy.

Japan

In an interview with Joshua J. McElwee of the *National Catholic Reporter*, 4 August 2011, Bishop Paul Otsuka of the Kyoto diocese, spoke in advance of the annual gathering in Hiroshima to commemorate the dropping of the atom bomb, sixty-six years ago. He said that this event takes on a new significance in the light of the accident at Fukushima. As a result, he felt that it is an appropriate time for the Japanese people to reflect on their relationship with nuclear power. The bishop referred to a letter sent from the Tokyo diocese to the entire Japanese Catholic Church. He wrote that Japan, 'which is the only country in the world to have been attacked with atomic weapons [now] stands in danger of becoming a country fundamentally damaged because of atomic energy generation'.[23]

The military use of atomic weapons and the impact of the nuclear accident at Fukushima calls on the Japanese to 'discern

---

22. Norimitu Onishi, 'A Nuclear Plant, and a Dream, Fizzles,' *The New York Times*, 13 February 2012. http://www.nytimes.com/2012/ 02/14/world/asia/bataan-nuclear-plant-never-opened-now-a-tourism-site.html.

23. Joshua J. McElwee, 'Nearing Hiroshima Day, Japanese bishop calls for discernment on nuclear energy,' *National Catholic Reporter*, 4 August 2011, http://ncronline.org/print/26025.

whether atomic energy, which threatens mankind and the environment, comes within the acceptable limits of our legitimate use of science and technology'.[24] Bishop Otsuka has called for discernment about nuclear energy use and a new approach to how we use energy across the globe.

In the interview, the bishop was asked for his reflections about the continuing disaster at the Fukushima nuclear power plant. In reply he stated:

> I wanted to write about nuclear energy because the damage from March's accident at the Fukushima plant continues. And many people sincerely wonder if it is possible for humankind to use nuclear energy safely. Until the incident, we believed it was possible for humankind to use our nuclear knowledge for peaceful use safely. It is good to use our nuclear knowledge for peaceful use if we have perfect technology to protect our planet. But this incident shows this is impossible. The perfect technical system is impossible.
>
> I and many other Japanese bishops started to think about this issue anew. I wanted to write about it from a Christian viewpoint. Pope John Paul II said in many documents that humankind has to be very careful how it uses technology. Generally speaking, God has given us inspiration to invent new technology. This does not mean we should have unlimited progress. We are not perfect. Although at this point we cannot say clearly that we should never use nuclear energy, we need a chance to seriously consider this issue.[25]

Like the German people, the bishop believes that the Japanese should also stop using nuclear energy, even if it takes a long time to wind down their nuclear power plants. He was adamant that the Japanese need to think about producing energy in a different way. He also made the point that renewable forms of energy ought to be promoted. The more fundamental issue is that

24. Ibid.
25. Ibid.

'modern society is addicted to energy. It's like a drug. People automatically assume we need more energy.'[26]

The bishop continued, 'so, from the point of view of the evangelical life, the modern world has to stop and take this chance to seriously consider our use of energy. Even though solar energy is unlimited, why do we need such a huge amount of energy?' He questioned whether progress was always a good thing and said that people must consider opting for a more simple lifestyle which will mean using much less energy. He is adamant that we have to completely change our thinking on how we use and produce energy.[27] 'Take for example the Amish people in the United States. They have a very different lifestyle. They use very little energy, I think. Their lifestyle is an extreme example, but perhaps it is a good example to some degree. It shows that a new type of lifestyle is possible. We cannot force people to live that lifestyle, but we have to acknowledge that there should be limits.'[28]

On 8 November 2011, the Catholic bishops in Japan called for an end to nuclear power generation. During a press conference at Motoderakoji Cathedral in Sendai City, they launched a document entitled, 'End Nuclear Energy Now: Facing the Tragedy of the Fukushima Daiichi Nuclear Plant Disaster.' Five bishops were present in person as representatives of the Catholic Bishops' Conference of Japan (CBCJ). They addressed their message to 'all those living in Japan'.[29] I include the full text of the pastoral letter in the appendix.

The Holy See on Nuclear Power

It seems very strange to me that the Vatican, which in other spheres preaches a pro-life ethic, should endorse civilian nuclear power. At the International Atomic Energy Agency (IAEA), in September 1982, Mgr Mario Peressin, the Vatican representative at the IAEA at the time, supported the civilian use of nuclear power. In his address he stated that:

---

26. Ibid.
27. Ibid.
28. Ibid.
29. 'End nuclear power now, say bishops,' http://www.ucanews.com/2011/11/10/end-nuclear-power-now-say-bishops/print.

The peaceful uses of nuclear energy had both advantages and disadvantages. The advantages of the very application of nuclear energy, whether in agriculture, food preservation, medicine or hydrology were widely recognised. The most important sector, however, was that of energy production for industrial and domestic use at a time when energy sources were becoming increasingly rare and when energy production costs were rising. Nuclear power could contribute to the economic development of the Third World countries and could help prevent the dangerous phenomena of deforestation and desertification due to excessively intensive exploitation of non-renewable energy sources. The benefits of peaceful use of nuclear energy should thus be extended to all countries, in particular to developing countries.

The use of nuclear power did, however, involve risks, associated either with accidents which might arise at nuclear power stations or with the storage of radioactive waste. Certain groups of naïve idealists and even certain personalities from the scientific, political, cultural or religious worlds condemn the use of nuclear power simply for that reason. It seemed more realistic not to overlook any effort to guarantee the safe operation of power stations and the safe disposal of waste and to minimise thereby the risks incurred on the understanding that, as with any human enterprise it was impossible to eliminate them totally.[30]

The best that can be said about this speech, in the light of Fukushima, is that the Vatican's position is very naïve. It is also very much out of step with statements from bishops or bishops' conferences in places where nuclear power plants are a burning issue.

A decade later, Archbishop Donato Squicciarini went even further and stated that the Holy See believes that all possible efforts should be made to extend to all countries, especially

---

30. International Atomic Energy Agency, General Conference, 26th regular session, 20–24 September 1982, record of the twentieth plenary meeting held at the Jeue Hofburg, Vienna.

developing ones, the benefits contained in the peaceful use of nuclear power.[31]

In a book entitled *A Modern Approach To the Protection of the Environment*, which emerged from a Study Week organised by the Pontifical Academy of the Sciences from 2 to 7 November 1987, many of the speakers were in favour of promoting nuclear power. Umberto Colombio, an Italian scientist (1927-2006) and Ugo Farinelli (Lecturer at the Italian Association of Energy Economics – IAEE) claimed that opposition to nuclear power stems from 'a form of fundamentalism which must be taken into consideration' and that 'in normal operating conditions, nuclear energy is probably the most environmentally-friendly form of energy. Pollution of the environment is extremely small and well controlled.'[32]

This position was echoed in an address to the 38th Regular Session of the International Atomic Energy Agency (IAEA) in Vienna given by Mgr Mario Zenari from the Vatican Secretariat of State in September 1994. In defence of nuclear energy, he said that the controls which are in place for nuclear energy are more sensitive and stringent than for any other energy source.

In 2006, twenty years after Chernobyl, Cardinal Renato Martino, the president of the Pontifical Council for Justice and Peace, invited many scientists to attend a seminar in the Vatican which supported the development of nuclear energy for civilian use. The speakers included Didier Louvat, from the IAEA in Vienna; the Ukrainian Health Minister Yuriy Polyachenko; Professor Wolfgang Platino of Roma Tre University; and Julio Medina de Armas of the Cuban programme for the children of Chernobyl.

In his concluding remarks, Cardinal Martino confirmed that the Holy See supported 'the continuing research on nuclear

---

31. 'Wise atomic energy plan is needed,' Archbishop Squicciarini address (to the) International Atomic Energy Conference in Vienna, *L'Osservatore Romano*, 30 September 1991, p. 3.
32. Umberto Colombo and Ugo Farninelli, 'Environmental Risks in the Production and Conservation of Energy and the Problems of Social Acceptability,' *A Modern Approach to the Protection of the Environment*, (edited by G.B. Marini-Bettolo) Pontificia Academia Scientiarum, MCMSXXXIX, pp. 89–90.

energy for civilian ends, so rich in technical, cultural and political applications'.[33] The cardinal also continued to articulate the Vatican's dismissive attitude towards those who are opposed to nuclear power by stating that, 'the seminar has taught us that nuclear energy must not be seen, as it often is, through the spectacles of ideological prejudice but with the look of intelligence, human rationality and science, accompanied by the wise exercise of prudence, in view of carrying out the integral and solidaristic development of the human person and nations.'[34]

This Vatican's support for nuclear power continued right up until 2009. At 'The Ministerial Conference on Nuclear Energy in the 21st Century' in Beijing on 21 April 2009, the Vatican representative, Monsignor Michael W. Banach, told the other delegates that, 'the nuclear sector can represent a great opportunity for the future. This explains the "nuclear renaissance" that is emerging at world level. This renaissance seems to offer horizons of development and prosperity.'[35]

During the three day conference in Beijing, Congressman Mark Cojuangco, who is the author of the Bill, HB4631, which is known as the Bataan Nuclear Power Plant Re-Commissioning Act 2008, sought a meeting with Monsignor Banach to find out where the Vatican stood on the issue of nuclear power. He came away from that meeting with the clear perception that the Vatican supported building nuclear power plants. 'The personal meeting with the Monsignor is especially important to me as a God-fearing individual and as a lawmaker, because our country is predominantly Catholic. I am elated and relieved, that I, as a Catholic, after all, am not violating any mandate of my church and that, as I have always believed, Pope Benedict XVI, is a well-informed, open-minded leader, who is hugely concerned for the welfare and well-being of the people, especially the poor.'[36]

33. www.zenit.org, 'Holy See Backs Civilian Use of Nuclear Energy,' Vatican City, 27 April 2006.
34. Ibid.
35. 'Intervention by the Holy See at the Ministerial Conference on Nuclear Energy in the 21st Century,' Beijing, 21 April 2009. www.vatican.va/roman_curia/secretariate_state/2009/document ministerial conference on nuclear energy.
36. 'Congressman Cojuangco Confirms Pope Stand on Nuke,' 28 April, 2009. http://bataan-npp.blogspot.com/2009/05/congressman-cojuangco-confirms-pope.html.

Cojuangco said that he personally sought out Monsignor Banach and related to him that the biggest challenge he faces in the Philippines as he proposes the rehabilitation of the Bataan Nuclear Plant is the opposition of the Diocese of Balanga to his bill, HB4631. Cojuangco sought validation from the Holy See's Representative for his interpretation of the Holy Father's previous statements: 'That the Pope is not-anti nuke and that the Vatican not only supports the mandate of the IAEA for the development of nuke technology for medicine but also for power generation as well.'[37] Also clarified with Monsignor Banach was the Congressman's interpretation of what the Holy Father and Cardinal Renato Martino had previously said: 'That humankind must be open minded about nuclear power for it may be instrumental in uplifting our condition, especially, that of the poor.'

Congressman Cojuangco specifically asked: 'Does the Holy Father mean nuclear technology only for medicine or for nuclear power as well? Was the Holy Father's statement only for Italy or for all of human kind?' To which Monsignor Banack responded, 'It is for nuclear power and it is for the whole of humankind.'[38]

A U-turn by the Vatican on Nuclear Power?

In a surprise development in September 2011, the Vatican did a U-turn on its traditional support for civilian nuclear power. Monsignor Michael Banach, the Vatican's representative to the International Atomic Energy Agency, told an IAEA gathering in Vienna on 20 September 2011, that 'this year's nuclear disaster in Japan has raised new concerns about the safety of nuclear plants around the world.'[39] The apparent change in the Vatican's position was prompted by the earthquake and tsunami which claimed the lives of 24,000 people in Japan in March 2011 and triggered an explosion at the nuclear power plant in Fukushima.

---

37. Ibid.
38. Ibid.
39. 'Vatican official says Japan nuclear crisis signals global problem,' submitted by NUCBIZ on 1 October 2011, http://www.nucpros.com/content/vatican-official-says-japan-nuclear-crisis-signals-globalproblem. 'Future of nuclear power in question,' The Universe, 9 October 2011, p. 12.

As a result of the accident, 200,000 people were evacuated from the area and the radioactive zone was said to be bigger than that created by the atomic bombs dropped on Hiroshima and Nagasaki in 1945, according to Monsignor Banach.[40]

He went on to question whether nuclear power plants should be built and operated in areas prone to earthquakes and whether plants that already exist in such areas should be shut down. 'The nuclear crisis in Fukushima-Daiichi raises many basic questions which need to be addressed, so as to improve the planning and management of nuclear power plants in accordance with the highest standards', he said.

'It revealed that the world is exposed to real and systematic risks, and not just hypothetical ones, with incalculable costs and the necessity of developing an international political coordination the likes of which have never been seen.'

'The long-term effects of the disaster include economical, medical and rebuilding costs in one of Japan's richest agricultural areas.'[41]

Monsignor Banach asked members about maintaining current nuclear plants properly and destroying old plants. 'Does nuclear fission technology, or the construction of new atomic power plants, or the continued operation of existing ones exclude human error in its phases of design, normal and emergency operation? To all these questions, there must also be added those concerning political will, technical capacity and necessary finances in order to proceed to the dismantling of many old nuclear reactors,' he said.[42]

Pope Benedict XVI mentioned the disaster at Fukushima in his address to the diplomats assigned to the Holy See in an address on 9 January 2012. 'Finally I would stress that education, correctly understood, cannot fail to foster respect for creation. We cannot disregard the grave natural calamities which in 2011 affected various regions of South-East Asia, or ecological disasters like that of the Fukushima nuclear plant in Japan. Environmental

---

40. Ibid.
41. Ibid.
42. Ibid.

protection and the connection between fighting poverty and fighting climate change are important areas for the promotion of integral human development. For this reason, I hope that, pursuant to the XVII session of the Conference of States which are Parties to the UN Convention on Climate Change recently concluded in Durban, the international community will prepare for the UN Conference on Sustainable Development ('Rio + 20') as an authentic 'family of nations' and thus with a great sense of solidarity and responsibility towards present and future generations.'[43]

Final Reflections

I began this book by referring to the activities of Prometheus in Greek mythology as illustrating the fascination humans have with energy. The hubris of Icarus, another figure from Greek mythology, provides an appropriate conclusion to a book on the dangers of nuclear energy. Icarus, the son of Daedalus, dared to fly too close to the sun on wings fashioned from feathers and wax. His father had been imprisoned by King Minos of Crete within the walls of his own invention, the Labyrinth. Daedalus was not willing to be held captive in this way, so he used technological skills to create a flying machine to escape. He made two pairs of wings by using wax to glue feathers to a wooden frame. He gave one pair to his son, Icarus, but he warned the boy not to fly too close to the sun because the wax would melt and he would fall and be killed. But Icarus was so intoxicated by his ability to fly that he forgot his father's warning. The feathers came loose and Icarus plunged to his death in the sea. Nuclear power is born out of the same hubris and arrogance shown by Icarus. We feel we can tame this dangerous technology without any negative consequences.

The book began by examining in detail what happened on 11 March 2011 at the Fukushima Daiichi nuclear plant when it was hit by an earthquake which registered 9 on the Richter scale. This was followed about forty minutes later by a fifty-foot high

---

43. Vatican City, 9 January 2012 (Zenit.org). Here is a Vatican translation of the New Year's address Benedict XVI gave today to the members of the diplomatic corps accredited to the Holy See. http://mail.google.com/mail/?tab=wm#inbox/134c666a67483d15.

tsunami which knocked out the back-up generators at the nuclear plant and cut off the cooling water to the reactors. Three of the six reactors were damaged. The following day, an explosion at Reactor 1 released a plume of radioactive isotopes such as caesium and iodine into the atmosphere. There were explosions also at Reactors 2 and 3, and contaminated water was released into the Pacific Ocean. In chapter 1 and 2, I give a host of examples of a totally incompetent response to the unfolding crisis from both the utility Tokyo Electric Power Company (Tepco) and the various Departments of the Japanese government. Tepco and the Japanese government attempted to minimise and cover up the extent of the problem, ostensibly so that people would not panic. This tendency to cover-up, play down and lie about accidents at nuclear plants, is not confined to Japan. It is now clear that Japan and the world was within a hair's breadth of a much more serious nuclear meltdown if the Tepco workers had been withdrawn from the stricken power plant.

In chapter 3, I give details of how the Fukushima Daiichi accident has affected the attitude of other countries to developing or continuing to use nuclear power. Just when it seemed to many proponents of nuclear power that the public had forgotten the impact of the accident at Three Mile Island in the US and Chernobyl in Ukraine, the disaster at Fukushima Daiichi has focused global attention on the problems posed by nuclear power plants. Germany, Italy and Switzerland have decided not to build any new nuclear power plants and to wind-down the power plants which are currently operating in their countries. Britain, the US and China plan to continue building nuclear power plants. I also include the nuclear ambitions of many countries in the Middle East, Africa and Asia.

In chapters 4 and 5 on 'Light-touch Regulation' and 'Nuclear Power, A History of Cover-ups, Deception and Incompetence', I give many examples of how the authorities in Russia (the former Soviet Union), Britain, the US and France have followed similar paths in attempting to ensure that the public does not really know what happens in a nuclear power plant when serious accidents happen. Often the nuclear regulatory authorities, which were put in place to protect the public, are colonised by the corporations which operate the reactors. When this happens, the welfare of the public is often forgotten.

China has decided to push through with an aggressive building programme for nuclear power plants, despite the fact that seismic activity is constantly taking place in that country and that some of the earthquakes in China in recent times have registered at more than 8 on the Richter scale. On seismic grounds alone, the Chinese authorities ought to have major concerns about the safety of nuclear power plants, but the fact that China is opting for older nuclear technology gives us further grounds for concern. In chapter 3, I quoted a question raised by a senior scientist, He Zuoxiu, 'Are we really ready for this giddy speed (of nuclear power development)? I think not – we're seriously under-prepared, especially on the safety front.'

In chapter 6, I argue that nuclear power is very expensive when everything, such as decommissioning and storing nuclear waste, is included in the cost. The cost of nuclear power and renewable forms of energy is the focus of chapter 8. On almost all indices, renewable energy comes out on top. The problem with nuclear energy is that it is costly, dangerous and long-lasting. If billions of euro are poured into building nuclear reactors in the next decades, countries that build these plants will be saddled with them for over one hundred years. Renewable energy, on the other hand, is much more flexible. The cost of many forms of renewable energy, especially photovoltaic, is dropping each year, just as the price of computers and mobile phones dropped in the past decade so that, within a few years, it will be more cost-effective when compared with fossil fuel and nuclear-generated energy.

Chapter 9 outlines how the Catholic Church has viewed nuclear power during the past few decades. Almost every national conference of bishops has rejected nuclear power. Among these countries are Canada, Germany, Korea, India, the Philippines and especially, Japan. I have included the complete pastoral letter from the Bishops of Japan in the appendix.

Ironically, the Holy See had been promoting civilian nuclear energy for decades. I presume that one of the reasons for this is that the Vatican was convinced by nuclear scientists that cheap nuclear energy was necessary, especially in developing countries, to provide energy for their growing populations. In reality, civilian nuclear power was never cheap, but it has been subsidised by governments in numerous ways, as has been outlined in this book. In October 2011, in response to the Fukushima Daiichi disaster, it seems that the Holy See has now changed its policy on promoting nuclear energy. Nuclear power is neither cheap nor safe.

Mr Saori Kanesaki worked at the Fukushima Daiichi nuclear power plant. His job was to give guided tours of the plant to visitors. He was one of the 16,000 inhabitants of the town of Tomioka who were driven from their homes by what happened in March 2011. He told Justin McCurry of *The Guardian*, 'Before the accident it was my job to tell visitors that nuclear power was safe. But given the situation, if I were to tell them that now … I would be lying.'[44]

Like Icarus, nuclear energy is grounded in human hubris, and the belief that we can tame and use such dangerous energy sources is extremely misguided. The consequences of nuclear accidents, as we have seen in both Chernobyl and Fukushima Daiichi continues for decades as people are forced from their homes with very little possibility of returning within twenty or thirty years. There are many alternative sources of energy and ways of delivering energy. Humans would be well-advised to devote their creative abilities to developing these clean sources of energy.

---

44. Justin McCurry, 'Fukushima, a year on: 3,000 workers take on the twisted steel and radiation,' *The Guardian*, 28 February 2012. http://www.guardian.co.uk/environment/2012/feb/28/fukushima-workers-twisted-steel-radiation/print.

APPENDIX

Pastoral Letter of the Japanese Bishops on Nuclear Energy

The accident in the Fukushima Daiichi Nuclear Plant triggered by the Great Eastern Japan Earthquake contaminated the ocean and land by radiation, and tragically disrupted the daily life of an enormous number of people. Even now, almost one hundred thousand people are evacuated from the neighbouring area of the nuclear plant, and numerous people are forced to live in fear and anxiety.

With regard to the pros and cons of nuclear plants, we, Japanese bishops, expressed in our message 'Reverence for Life – A Message for the Twenty-First Century from the Catholic Bishops of Japan,' as follows:

> It has provided a totally new source of energy for humanity, but as we can see in the destruction of human life in a moment in Hiroshima and Nagasaki, the disaster at Chernobyl and the life-threatening criticality accident at Tokaimura, it also has the potential to pass huge problems on to future generations. To use it effectively, we need the wisdom to know our limits and exercise the greatest care. In order to avoid tragedy, we must develop safe alternative means of producing energy.

The 'tragedy' in this message was brought about by nothing less than the accident in the Fukushima Daiichi Nuclear Plant. This nuclear disaster wiped out the 'safety myth', which was created because people put too much trust in science and technology without having 'the wisdom to know our limits'.

In the message 'Reverence for Life', we, Japanese bishops could not go so far as to urge the immediate abolishment of nuclear plants. However, after facing the tragic nuclear disaster in Fukushima, we regretted and reconsidered such attitude. And now, we would like to call for the immediate abolishment of all the power plants in Japan.

With regard to the immediate abolishment of nuclear plants, some people voice concerns about energy shortage. There are also various challenges such as the reduction of carbon dioxide. However, most important of all, we as members of the human race, have responsibilities to protect all life and nature as God's creation, and to pass on a safer and more secure environment to future generations. In order to protect life, which is so precious, and beautiful we must not focus on economic growth by placing priority on profitability and efficiency, but decide at once to abolish nuclear plants.

Because of the prediction that a new disaster will occur due to another earthquake or tsunami, all of the fifty-four nuclear plants in Japan are at risk of horrific accidents like the latest one. Therefore, in order to prevent human-generated calamities associated with natural disasters as much as possible, it is essential to eliminate nuclear plants.

Although nuclear plants have been supplying energy in the context of 'peaceful use' to society until now, they have also released an enormous amount of radioactive waste such as plutonium. We are going to place the custodial responsibility of these dangerous wastes on future generations for centuries to come. We must consider this matter to be an ethical issue.

Nuclear power has been encouraged by national policies up to now. As a result, natural energy has fallen behind in development and popularity. We urge that the national policies be changed to place top priority on development and implementation of natural energy, which will also contribute to reducing carbon dioxide. On the other hand, it takes a long time and enormous labor to decommission a nuclear plant. Therefore, the decommissioning of reactors and the disposal of radioactive waste must be conducted with extreme caution.

Indeed, electricity is essential for our lives today. However, what is important is to amend our ways of general life by changing the lifestyles that excessively depend on electricity.

Japan has its culture, wisdom and tradition that have long co-existed with nature. Religions such as Shinto and Buddhism are also based on the same spirit. Christianity has the spirit of poverty as well. Therefore, Christians have an obligation to bear genuine witness to the Gospel especially through the ways of life expected by God; 'simplicity of life, the spirit of prayer, charity towards all, especially towards the lowly and the poor, obedience and humility, detachment and self-sacrifice'.

We should choose anew a simple and plain lifestyle based on the spirit of the Gospel, in cases like saving electricity. We live in the hope that science and technology will develop and advance based on the same spirit. These attitudes will surely lead to a safer and more secure life without nuclear plants.energy, which will also contribute to reducing carbon dioxide. On the other hand, it takes a long time and enormous labour to decommission a nuclear plant.[1]

---

1. http://www.cbcj.catholic.jp/eng/edoc/111108.html.

Index

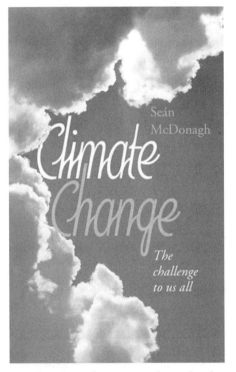

This book is a timely examination of the case for nuclear power in the aftermath of the Fukushima disaster. It is particularly strong in placing the scientific arguments in the context of how regulation of the industry has been weak and dominated by political self-interest. The argument throughout is informed by a thorough knowledge of experiences throughout the world as well as by ethical considerations.

Dr Peadar Kirby